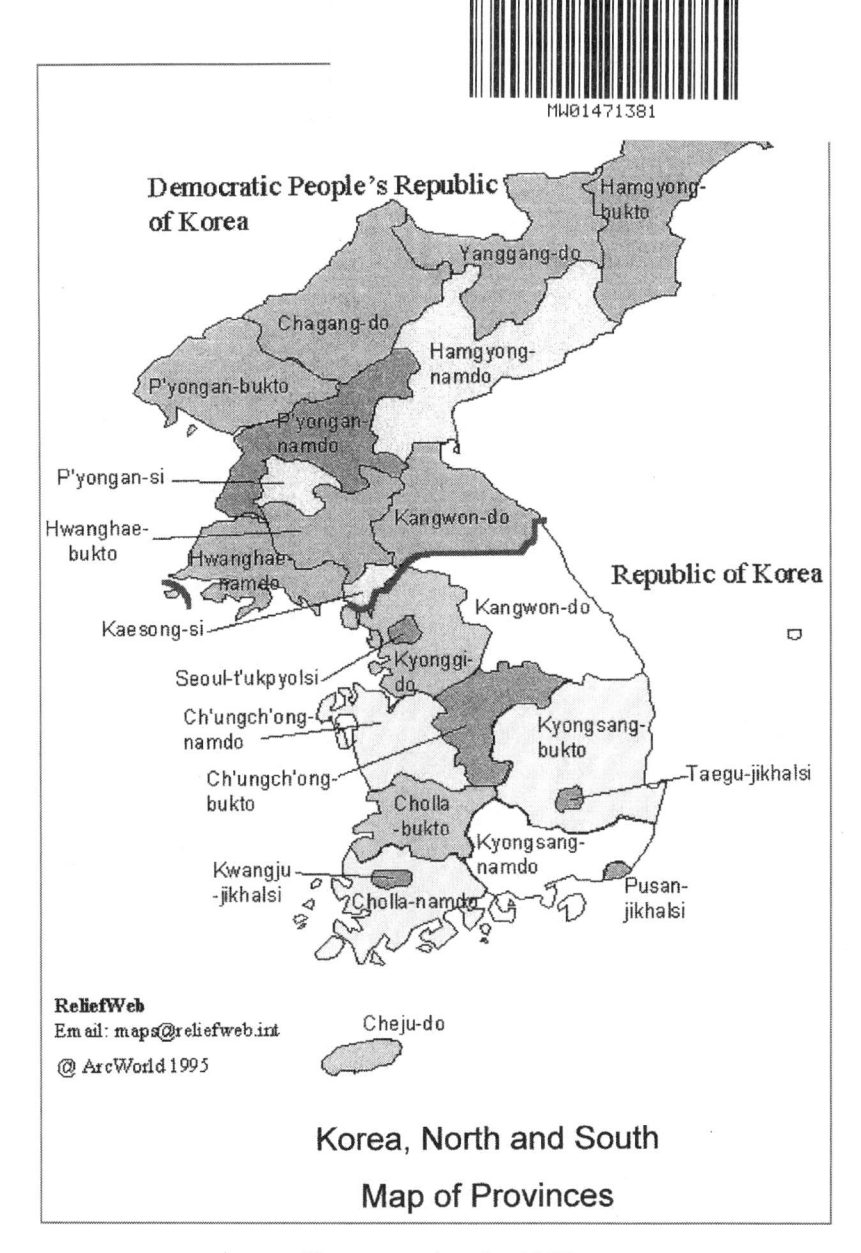

Korean peninsula, 1995

Map provided courtesy of the ReliefWeb Map Centre, UN Office for the Coordination of Humanitarian Affairs. It can be found online at: **http://reliefweb.int/map/republic-korea/korean-peninsula-provinces**. The boundaries and names shown and the designations used on this map do not imply official endorsement or acceptance by the United Nations

KOREA, ARE YOU AT PEACE?

*Tales of Two Women Travelers
in a Troubled Land*

J. A. V. Simson

abbott press®
A DIVISION OF WRITER'S DIGEST

Copyright © 2013 J. A. V. Simson.

All rights reserved. No part of this book may be used or reproduced by any means, graphic, electronic, or mechanical, including photocopying, recording, taping or by any information storage retrieval system without the written permission of the publisher except in the case of brief quotations embodied in critical articles and reviews.

Abbott Press books may be ordered through booksellers or by contacting:

Abbott Press
1663 Liberty Drive
Bloomington, IN 47403
www.abbottpress.com
Phone: 1-866-697-5310

Because of the dynamic nature of the Internet, any web addresses or links contained in this book may have changed since publication and may no longer be valid. The views expressed in this work are solely those of the author and do not necessarily reflect the views of the publisher, and the publisher hereby disclaims any responsibility for them.

ISBN: 978-1-4582-1038-8 (sc)
ISBN: 978-1-4582-1037-1 (hc)
ISBN: 978-1-4582-1036-4 (e)

Library of Congress Control Number: 2013911480

Printed in the United States of America.

Abbott Press rev. date: 8/8/2013

This book is dedicated to the Korean people, particularly to the women of Korea, many of whom were kind and helpful when I was in their land. I would also like to honor Park Geun-hye, the first woman president of her country. Stand strong.

TABLE OF CONTENTS

Prologue. xi

Section I: Culture Shock In The Hermit Kingdom. 1

Chapter 1.   Arriving In Asia 3
Chapter 2.   Buying A Car In A Buddhist Eatery. 12
Chapter 3.   Three Foreign Cultures 21
Chapter 4.   The Demilitarized Zone (DMZ) 31

Section II: Into The Korean Backcountry. 41

Chapter 5.   Out Of Town And Into The Mountains. 43
Chapter 6.   Temples, Tombs, And Time 57
Chapter 7.   Cars, Bars, And Military Bases 66
Chapter 8.   Monsoon. 74
Chapter 9.   Taegu, Where The Livin' Ain't Easy 84
Chapter 10. Southern Comfort, Korean Style. 96

Section III: Reflections On The Korean Way. 101

Chapter 11. Language, Class, And Culture 103
Chapter 12. Religion, Belief, And Hope 114
Chapter 13. Women In Korea 125
Chapter 14. Environmentally Friendly Korea 137
Chapter 15. Lasting Impressions, Land Of Morning Calm 142

Appendix: Overview of Korean History 151

Transliterations of Korean Words 165

Suggested Readings 167

Acknowledgements 169

Endnotes 173

Index.. 177

LIST OF ILLUSTRATIONS

Front cover photo	Tower at DMZ
Front piece map	Korean peninsula, '95
page 11	Huge Buddha at Gagwonsa
page 20	The CAR, apartment building, Songtan
page 30	Eaves on Buddhist temple
page 34	DMZ
page 40	Tunnel entrance, DMZ
page 56	Soraksan National Park
page 60	Mounds and mountains, Kyongju
page 65	School children at Kyongju
page 85	Street scene in Taegu
page 95	The Daewoo in the snow, Taegu
page 100	Lava gnomes, Chejudo
page 113	Yangban country village
page 124	Buddhist monk at Pulguksa
page 141	Gardens between apartment buildings, Songtan
page 150	Gentle mountains in south-eastern Korea
page 164	Turtle ship replica, cherry blossoms, Chinhae
Back piece map	Map, Korean itineraries – Bishop (circles) & Simson (squares)
Back cover photo	Author, steps to Sokkuram

PROLOGUE

What I really wanted to do after retiring from the Medical University was to travel and have someone else pay for it. When a call came that summer from the University of Maryland, University College (UMUC) Overseas Division offering a teaching job in Asia that fall, I made hasty arrangements—house, mail, bills— and left Charleston, South Carolina for Korea, a part of the globe I had never seen before. UMUC had offered me a teaching position overseas twice before, but other commitments had gotten in the way. I knew if I declined this time, there would be no fourth offer.

For two years I taught on American military bases and lived among the Korean people—on the economy as it's called. When I use the word Korea, I mean South Korea, or the Republic of Korea (ROK). Historically, Korea extended the entire length of the peninsula that lies between the island nation of Japan and mainland China. It became divided into North Korea and South Korea shortly after World War II and has been since then a potential political tinderbox.

While in Korea I became increasingly aware of deep differences between Eastern and Western cultures. I came to realize the prime importance of respect—even more than trust—in interpersonal relations in Korea. I also experienced the problematic nature of an American military presence in another sovereign nation. In part, *Korea, Are you at Peace?* is an attempt to record this unfolding awareness.

This book also narrates my efforts to understand the tragic

history of the Korean peninsula during the twentieth century. Late nineteenth century Korea was the last Asian country to be penetrated by the West. Soon thereafter, the horrors of the twentieth century overwhelmed the country: Japanese occupation, two world wars, and a national schism, with Korea a pawn in a power struggle between East and West.

As a foil for this historical approach, I compare my observations and insights with those of another Western woman, a Victorian travel writer named Isabella Bird Bishop, who had explored Korea a century previously.

In Korea, I purchased a book entitled *Korea's Cultural Roots* by Dr. Jon Carter Covell.[1] In it the author describes a "Scotswoman," Mrs. Bishop who, at age sixty three, traveled around Korea on her own in the 1890s. Covell recommended "...that the reader get a copy of this book, to contrast the pitiful conditions of life in the Hermit Kingdom of the 1890's with the bustling prosperity and modernization of today." However, the author provided neither the title of the book nor its publisher, and Mrs. Bishop's name was not given in full. After returning to the United States and pulling together some recollections of Korea, I decided to investigate. Who was this Mrs. Bishop?

A Google search turned up several references to Isabella Lucy Bird Bishop and to her written work, including a book on Korea entitled *Korea and Her Neighbors*.[2] It happened to be available in facsimile edition, and I purchased a copy. I soon became fascinated by Bishop and her Korean observations and stories, and I realized that her experiences in Korea contrasted with mine in almost every respect. Incorporating her stories into this narrative allowed me to frame my experiences in Korea against the backdrop of a Victorian lady's travels in an unknown land.

Isabella Bird Bishop was already a world traveler and respected travel writer, known to most as Isabella Bird, when she undertook a lengthy sojourn to Korea and nearby regions of China, Russia and Japan (1894 – '96). At that time, Korea was referred to as the Hermit Kingdom of Asia for its resistance to interaction with the West.[3] Bishop was there when Korea was wrenched from its isolated, traditional culture and cast into the larger world through trial by fire. Our two journeys frame a long, dark century of devastation and chaos for this beleaguered country and its people. It was during the brutal twentieth century that the Korean peninsula suffered invasion by neighbors, a long, oppressive Japanese occupation, and two dreadful wars—World War II and the Korean War.

Indeed, the itinerary and timing of the last part of Mrs. Bishop's journey was determined largely by political events, particularly the war between Japan and China of 1894 – '95. Ironically, that brief war was fought to determine which of those two nations had the right to protect Korea's independence, which effectively meant the right to exercise suzerainty over the country. Japan won the war, took political control of Korea, and ruled it as a Japanese colony for half a century. After World War II, the country was split—by an agreement between the U.S. and the USSR—into North Korea and South Korea. Shortly after the great powers withdrew in 1948, the Korean War convulsed the peninsula for another three years.

That somber past continues in the part of the peninsula north of the 38th parallel, the Democratic People's Republic of Korea (DPRK, North Korea), whose citizens remain locked in a totalitarian cultural nightmare. The Republic of Korea (South Korea) by contrast, has finally achieved a degree of peace, crowned by a new and vibrant economy. It is considered one of Asia's four "Little Tigers," small, economically successful countries of East Asia: Hong Kong, South Korea, Singapore and Taiwan.

Despite a century of war and turmoil, Koreans retain their traditional greeting, *Annyong haseyo,* or 'Are you at peace?' This greeting reflects the Buddhist heritage of Korea, in which peace and harmony are expected to accompany wisdom and right behavior. Peace is a primary cultural value for Koreans—both as personal, internal peace through their Buddhist heritage and as public peace in the Confucian tradition. But peace is something that has eluded the Korean peninsula in recent history, and it is still tenuous. American military troops and materiel in the South still face off against the threat of invasion—even nuclear attack—from the North.

My job with UMUC was to teach biology on American military installations throughout South Korea. The people with whom I interacted in classes were mostly U.S. soldiers, although military contractors and Korean nationals with military connections sometimes enrolled. Outside the classroom, I spent some time with Koreans and with UMUC faculty. But mostly, I was on my own, wandering through towns and traveling around the countryside whenever possible, getting to know the country and its people. Like Bishop, I was able to see Korea in a way experienced by few Westerners.

Isabella Bishop and I each recorded our experiences from a deeply personal perspective. She was enthralled by the countryside but largely annoyed by what she perceived as the medieval behavior of its nineteenth-century inhabitants. I focused ever more sharply on the heartbreak of twentieth century Korea and the looming potential tragedy of the present century.

Bishop provided more informational details on the country when describing her travels than I have, but my narrative has the advantage of a unique historical perspective. I have woven her late-nineteenth-century experiences into my recollections and reflections on contemporary Korea at the beginning of the twenty-first century.

My main motive for sharing these impressions of Korea is to offer insight into a country that comparatively few Westerners have visited, that has had few literary champions, and that rarely makes the news unless North Korea rattles its missiles. Several chapters highlight the inevitable dissonances that occur when Koreans and American military personnel interact. Most Americans who have actually spent time on the Korean peninsula, especially G.I.s of the Korean War, are reluctant to talk about their experiences. Events and impressions are reported as I recorded and remembered them, but names of all those I met in Korea, both American and Korean, have been changed.

The front piece map shows Korean provinces and metropolitan areas as they were named when I was in the country (1999 – 2001). The transliterations of Korean place names are those most commonly used at that time. Newer transliterations are now standard; these can be found in a table following the Appendix (p. 165). The back piece map illustrates Isabella Bishops itinerary (circles) as well as the places I visited (squares).

It was worth the effort to penetrate this small jewel of a country that could be considered the Switzerland of Asia. Charming, mountainous, and inhabited by honest, industrious, and fiercely independent people, South Korea and its energetic population do not deserve the intellectual neglect of Western culture.

SECTION I:

Culture Shock In The Hermit Kingdom

Isabella Lucy Bird Bishop, a Victorian travel writer, and I, a biologist under contract with the U.S. military, arrived in Korea by way of Japan—she in 1894 and I in 1999. We were both seasoned world travelers and women of the same age when we came to explore Korea, a country that was hardly on anyone's travel wish-list. We both experienced culture shock despite many prior experiences of foreign cultures; Korea, the erstwhile Hermit Kingdom, was unlike any country either of us had visited. After initial dismay and disorientation, we both managed to accommodate to our surroundings—she with the aid of missionaries and the British consulate, and I with help from UMUC Overseas Division and the U.S. military abroad. Our separate journeys bracketed the twentieth century, a century of deep cultural dislocation for Korea and its people.

Chapter 1

ARRIVING IN ASIA

When Isabella Lucy Bird Bishop arrived in Korea in the winter of 1894, the port of Pusan was crawling with Japanese officials, merchants, and military men. She was already a seasoned traveler, who had visited and written books on North America, Australia, the Hawaiian (Sandwich) Islands, Japan, and India. Indeed, she was an exceptional nineteenth century British woman, who supported herself by the sale of her travel books. She had been transported to Pusan from Nagasaki aboard a Japanese steamship, the *Higo Maru*. The large number of Japanese operating in this Korean port might have signaled that something was amiss, but in early chapters of her book, she does not dwell on the paradox.

Pusan, which Bishop transliterated as 'Fusan' throughout *Korea and Her Neighbors* (and which is now generally transliterated 'Busan') is the major port in southeastern Korea. It was the city from which General MacArthur mounted the defense of South Korea after the invasion from the North in 1950 that started the Korean War. When Isabella Bishop was there, Pusan was controlled by the Japanese, who had made it a treaty port in 1876, using a form of gunboat diplomacy similar to that previously exerted by Western powers on Japan and other Asian countries. This was part of a long-term Japanese strategy to control shipping and trade in eastern Asia. By the end of her stay in Korea, Bishop appeared to be sympathetic to

Japanese imperial impulses in Asia, perhaps reflecting the British imperialistic worldview of her time.

When Isabella Bishop initially arrived in the port, her impressions of Koreans were positive. She found the white-suited Korean a *"novelty, and while resembling neither the Chinese nor the Japanese...is much better looking than either, and his physique is far finer than that of the latter."*[4] She also declared that *"mentally, the Koreans are liberally endowed... The foreign teachers bear willing testimony to their mental adroitness and quickness of perception."*[5]

I also arrived in Korea by way of Japan, seriously jet-lagged and disoriented, having spent more than twenty hours in the air from Charleston, South Carolina to Los Angeles and then across the Pacific. I was one of fifteen faculty members newly recruited to teach college courses to American military personnel in Asia for UMUC in the fall of 1999. We flew into Tokyo for our initial orientation to the unfamiliar Asian culture and to the almost equally unfamiliar American military culture within which we would be working.

Following three days of orientation in Japan, those of us teaching in Korea flew on to Seoul to complete training on the Korean peninsula. I was to teach biology at Osan Air Force Base (Osan AFB) near the town of Songtan, about forty miles south of Seoul. In Seoul, we filled out official documents and forms for military passes, heard lectures on Korean history and culture, and toured Seoul and the nearby countryside.

During that time, we made several trips to monuments, temples and museums within easy driving distance of Seoul. We spent one afternoon at Independence Hall, the national museum of culture in Chungchongnam-do. For those interested in language, *do* means 'region' in Korean. Another day we visited a temple boasting a huge statue of a sitting Buddha at Gagwonsa. To give an idea of the country's comfortable size, we were able to drive from Seoul, near the northern border of South Korea, to Gagwonsa, almost halfway to the southern tip of the country, eat lunch there, make a leisurely visit to the temple with its great seated Buddha, and drive back to Seoul that same evening.

Korean museums are fascinating, if not entirely foreign-tourist friendly; however, my favorite places to visit were Buddhist temples—colorful and highly decorated structures, peopled by drab, gray-garbed monks, who sometimes chanted with medieval monotony, beat drums like jazz musicians, and struck huge bell-like gongs with logs, but otherwise simply walked reverently around the temple grounds. Gardens adjacent to Buddhist temple grounds were probably the source of their food, as is true with monasteries in the West. Some temple grounds also offer accommodations to (paying) visitors who wish to experience the peace and quiet meditation found there. Some orders are even more entrepreneurial; we ate at a restaurant in Seoul that was run by Buddhist monks.

From Pusan, Bishop traveled by Japanese ship to Chemulpo, the name she uses throughout her book for the port of Inchon on the Western shore of the Korean peninsula. Located not far from the mouth of the Han River, this is the port nearest Seoul and the site of General MacArthur's surprise Inchon Landing in September, 1950 that turned the tide of the Korean War.

From Inchon, Bishop proceeded by *"chair"* (palanquin) to Seoul, thanks to arrangements made by a British official. She described the countryside in the vicinity of Seoul as charming. However, her impression of Seoul was distinctly negative. The city disturbed and disgusted her.

> *"I know Seoul by day and night, its palaces and slums, its unspeakable meanness and faded splendors, its purposeless crowds, its medieval processions which, for barbaric splendor cannot be matched on earth, the filth of its crowded alleys, and its pitiful attempt to retain its*

> *manners, customs and identity as a capital of an ancient monarchy in the face of the host of disintegrating influences which are at work. . ."*[6]

I shared Bishop's distaste of Seoul and of other large Korean cities and looked forward to leaving the city as soon as possible. Nonetheless, that week in Seoul was an eye-opener. As it progressed, I began to develop a keen interest in Korean history and culture. The people and their customs aroused my sympathy, in part because of the ordeals they had suffered in the preceding century. The Korean peninsula has been a buffer between Japan and China for two millennia. Korea borrowed extensively from the Chinese, and contributed greatly to Japanese culture, although the Japanese are loath to admit it. Exhibits at Independence Hall made obvious the fierce cultural pride of Koreans and their equally intense desire for autonomy and abiding mistrust of the Japanese.

Isabella Bishop would not have recognized the Korea I saw those first few weeks in Asia. Wide streets clogged with cars; buildings reaching to the sky; women walking about by day. As time went by though, the afterglow of the ancient Hermit Kingdom seeped into my consciousness like cosmic background radiation. Deferential bowing; drums and gongs in somber Buddhist temples; mistrust of foreigners; wild, shamanistic dances by women in brightly colored, flowing silken robes; bowing and expressions of respect; the casual mistreatment of women.

One of the sites we visited during orientation week was a Korean Folk Village in Kyonggi-do, an idealized version of past village life. As a Michigan native, the site felt like a Korean version of Greenfield Village, the open-air Henry Ford museum in Dearborn. I wandered through the reconstructed, century-old shops and family compounds, each of which consisted of four or five buildings surrounding a central courtyard, often walled for privacy. The domiciles were neat and sparsely fitted out with mats, pottery, and low tables.

This idealized version of Korean country village life contrasted sharply with life in the villages Isabella Bishop described. She spent the greater part of a year traveling into the Korean backcountry by boat (*sampan*), cart, or horseback. There she saw mainly the poverty, squalor and confusion of life in villages along the way.

> *"The regular inn of the towns and large villages consists chiefly of a filthy courtyard full of holes and heaps, entered from the road by a tumble-down gateway. A gaunt black pig or two tethered by the ears, big yellow dogs routing in the garbage, and fowls, boys, bulls, ponies, mapu (horse handlers), hangers-on, and travelers' loads make up a busy scene...*
>
> *On one or two sides are ramshackle sheds, with rude, hollowed trunks in front, out of which the ponies suck the hot brown slush which sustains their strength and pugnacity... Low lattice doors filled in with dirty paper give access to a room, the mud floor of which is concealed by reed mats, usually dilapidated, sprinkled with wooden blocks which serve as pillows. Into this room are crowded mapu, travelers, and servants, the low residuum of Korean travel..."*[7]

During my backcountry meanderings, I happened upon a couple of small countryside villages that were certainly neater than those described by Bishop. I visited some of the same areas she did but arrived there by vastly different means. In late nineteenth-century Korea, the major vehicles of transportation outside of cities were boats, horses, and carts. Boats navigated the many waterways lacing the mountainous countryside; small, feisty Korean ponies carried travelers over winding mountain paths; and bull-carts trudged the muddy and rutted paths of the backcountry. I had the luxury of traveling primarily by car, train, or bus. The railways and major roads, while crowded, were reasonably well maintained.

To those who are receptive, solo travel in unfamiliar surroundings enhances sensitivity to sensory stimuli. It may be this heightened awareness that becomes addictive to the inveterate traveler, who wants to see, smell, hear and feel with an intensity normally dampened in familiar surroundings and in the company of others. The first few weeks in Korea were a bombardment of unfamiliar sensations. Everything around me was unfamiliar—sights were exotic, tastes and smells were strange, and sounds...well...the sounds were a cacophony I had to stretch my mind to contain and interpret.

The sights of the town I lived in, Songtan, contrasted sharply with my prior suburban American imagery. No one had a lawn, but gardens were everywhere. Plots of corn and beans surrounded houses, and melon vines grew up trellises and pillars that formed a part of the very structure of homes. An enchantingly colorful image I came upon during early meanderings was of mats laid neatly in front of homes along the roadway and covered with red peppers drying in the sun. It was late summer, leading into fall, and although the trees above were browning monotonously, the brilliant red mats below created the visual joy of a New England autumn.

The smells, too, were rich and densely organic. Behind my apartment building were two houses with roofs on a level with my balcony. When the frosted glass door to the balcony was open, I could see across garden patches below to *kim-chi* pots and clothes lines decorating the flat rooftops. Earthy, fermenting smells of kim-chi hung in the air, flavoring the ambient moisture and soot.

Kim-chi, the national condiment, is made from fermented vegetables, usually cabbage, like a Korean version of sauerkraut. It is laced with wild herbs, heavily spiked with red pepper. Its flavor and odor vary depending on the ingredients and the preparer, but the common version has an acrid smell with a sour and slightly bitter taste—a cross between beer, sauerkraut, horseradish, and red pepper. Sometimes it has putrid overtones, especially if fish are in the mix. Kim-chi is served with every meal, rather like ketchup in America, and it is eaten with almost everything except sweets. My favorite was radish kim-chi, a delicacy not served often. The condiment is stored in crockery pots on side patios or flat roofs of every Korean home. Ideally, at some stage of the fermentation process, the pot is buried underground to make the fermentation process anaerobic, which is not so easy with urban kim-chi production. Offers of kim-chi were a form of hospitality I learned to accept graciously, and I came to enjoy a bit of it with meals.

And then there were the sounds. The end of summer was hot in Songtan—oppressively hot and muggy—although probably no worse than Charleston would have been in late August without air-conditioning. Like most apartments and homes off-base, my apartment had no air-conditioner, so windows were left open to catch any chance breezes. Unfamiliar sounds rang through open windows. The loudest were from Osan airbase only a few blocks away. The shriek of jets and the thump-thump of helicopters reverberated in the still air. Shrill sirens announced emergency-system tests on base. Taps and anthems were blurred and muffled in the dense air.

From the streets and houses behind my apartment, urgent voices and distressed animal sounds carried through open windows. In the trees and grasses, insects whirred and tittered, especially, the buzz-saw screeching of cicadas; these sounded louder and more insistent than Charleston cicadas. A particularly noisy colony inhabited a poplar tree near the Education Center on base. It was almost deafening to walk beneath that tree when I first went to introduce myself to co-workers in the UMUC office and to pick up keys for a very cheap old car I had purchased with a fellow faculty member. For two or three days, the cicadas screeched and scolded every time I walked beneath that tree. Then a cold snap came and the tree fell silent. A few mornings later, cicadas were strumming their fierce trills again, so I knew the weather had warmed. However, a cold spell so early in autumn suggested that rumors of cold Korean winters were probably not idle.

Another unfamiliar sound thrumming through open windows and on the streets was, of course, the Korean language. Its guttural exclamations rang through the alleyways of Songtan, and a gentler version was exchanged on Osan airbase between Koreans, mostly women, who performed the everyday service work on base. They were secretaries, bank tellers, food servers at the Taco Bell or Antonio's Pizza, check-out clerks at the commissary and Base Exchange. With one another they spoke Korean; when they addressed customers (soldiers and contractors), they used English with variable success. Sometimes a G.I. or a contractor would make an angry or disparaging remark if he couldn't understand the slurred sentences of a woman hired to make on-base life easy. Insulting words, tones and gestures probably penetrated, but the soldiers' rudeness rarely perturbed the polite and deferential façade of service workers. It's hard to know how much ill will may have festered behind the polite demeanor. I never heard a woman answer back or defend herself against the rudeness, but it must have rankled in someone of a culture where respect is of paramount value.

In one of the buildings behind my apartment, the man of the family shouted a lot. Of course, I couldn't make out what he was saying—it often sounded simply like grunts that varied in pitch. Sometimes a woman would yell back; sometimes there was wailing; sometimes I could hear a child cry or a dog bark. One time I saw a man on his roof strike a woman; I assumed it was his wife. And one night I awoke to sounds of yelling and thumping and wailing that lasted for what seemed like half an hour. I had trouble going back to sleep, thinking about that not-so-distant drama and another woman's helplessness. As well as my own.

Huge Buddha at Gagwonsa

Chapter 2

BUYING A CAR IN A BUDDHIST EATERY

During orientation week in Seoul I bought a car. That is to say, John, another new faculty member, and I gave Sam, a veteran Marylander, $220 for an '88 Hyundai that Sam was desperately trying to unload. It all started in a dimly lit Buddhist restaurant where we had our final communal dinner of orientation week. We were drinking rice wine and eating a wild variety of mysterious vegetarian concoctions—mix-and-match versions of diced *this* with *that* sauce, some of it very hot—when a colleague across the table began to talk about a car he was trying to sell. Indeed, he *needed* to sell it because he had bought a new one and couldn't legally keep more than one car on base. In fact, his old car was parked illegally by the auto repair shop at the military base in Seoul. He thought he had a buyer, but the deal had fallen through. He claimed the sound system alone was worth $200.

John, sitting next to me and also destined for Osan, said, "Heck, I'll buy the sound system."

I turned to him and asked, "Why don't we go in halves and buy the car?"

He laughed. "Sure, why not."

Sam responded immediately. "It's a deal."

The next day, everyone in our group left for Osan except me.

My apartment wasn't ready, having apparently been abandoned in chaos by the previous tenant. I hung around the Education Center and got online in the computer room, where I saw Sam and asked him about the car. He was a bit vague and bleary-eyed, but he seemed to remember that he had offered to sell his old car for $200, and he really wanted to get rid of it. With a little prodding, he took me to see the vehicle and do a "test drive" around the parking lot. When I agreed to buy it, he helped me transfer the title on-base and obtain insurance off-base. The insurance cost more than the car itself. Before buying the car, I told Sam I would *not* drive it out of Seoul, and he agreed to deliver it to Osan.

The roads in Seoul may be better than they were when Isabella Bishop was there. But Seoul's streets are at least as confusing as those Bishop complained about, and they are jammed with cars whose drivers' daring and aggression rival New York taxi drivers on a very busy day. I gave Sam an extra twenty dollars for gas money to drive the car to Osan.

When I arrived at the airbase next day, THE CAR, in all its banged-up and rusted glory, was parked behind the Education Building. One of the women in the office gave me the keys. John was surprised that we really had a car and that it had happened so quickly. During those first few months in Korea, I taught classes at Osan AFB and Camp Humphreys, and the car took me and other colleagues back and forth to classes. It proved indispensable for carrying groceries and laundry and lab supplies on and off base at Osan. And it was generally reliable transportation to and from classes at Camp Humphreys, a military base near the town of Pyongt'aek, about half an hour south of Songtan.

Buying the car was the easy part; the hard part was finding roads that would take me where I wanted to go. The Korean road system consists of a main north-south throughway and other roads leading hither and thither—few of them connected directly to the main highway. Most Korean roads are ancient, having arisen as dirt wagon trails before the concept of grid work came into civilized consciousness. Thus, roads often fork off from other roads in a V or a Y or some other erratic geometry rather than intersecting at right angles.

This was evident in Isabella Bishop's description of the muddy cart tracks that passed for roads when she traveled the Korean backcountry, and even in Pusan, the major southern port of the peninsula. She also found the streets of Seoul abominable; most were dirt lanes and muddy alleyways, rutted and littered with garbage.

> "[A]n estimated quarter of a million people are living...chiefly in labyrinthine alleys, many of them not wide enough for two loaded bulls to pass, indeed barely wide enough for one man to pass a loaded bull, and further narrowed by a series of vile holes or green, slimy ditches, which receive the solid and liquid refuse of the houses, their foul and fetid margins being the favorite resort of half-naked children, begrimed with dirt...."[8]

Some old-timers teaching with UMUC in Korea told of difficulties getting about when roads were simply tracks of dirt and mud. The same awful mud roads were mentioned to me by American friends and a relative who were soldiers during the Korean War. Several contemporary roads were paved with the help of the U.S. military, in part for strategic purposes. It was only after the Korean War that motorized vehicles became an important part of Korean culture.

After arriving in Osan on a Thursday and appropriating the car, I realized I was scheduled to teach that following Monday at Camp Humphreys about twenty miles south of Osan. A military base bus ran between Osan and Humphreys, but its last scheduled departure from Humphreys was before the end of class-time, so the car seemed like the best option. However, I thought I had better figure out the route to drive between bases if I planned to take the car.

The next day, Friday afternoon, I took a base bus from Osan to Humphreys and tried to map out the way. Then I took the bus back, again trying to keep track of turns and landmarks in reverse. I also was given a hand-drawn map by a long-time faculty member. I told one of the Korean women in the UMUC office at Osan that I planned to drive to Camp Humphreys by myself on Saturday and would stop for help if I was lost. Her face took on a look of amused disparagement, and she said cryptically, "No help."

Sandy, another new faculty member also scheduled to teach at Humphreys the same evenings as I, came along in the car to help scope out the way. I had tracked the route from the gate behind the airbase—with its five or six turns on back roads—to the main highway, so that part of the trip went well. But the highway turn-off to Pyongt'aek was not marked as I expected, and we overshot by one exit. We got off at the following exit, got back onto the highway again, and exited correctly on the next try. I was feeling pretty confident.

However, I somehow hadn't recorded a V-fork that the bus must have taken. Did it seem like simply a curve? Things began to look unfamiliar. We found ourselves in a village I didn't recognize at all. We drove around and eventually found a large map of the area posted in a triangle near the village center. Of course, all writing was Korean, and I had not brought my Korean-English dictionary. Bad mistake and never again. Moreover, the map had no road numbers and was clearly designed for Korean tourists who wanted to find a local Buddhist temple or a hot springs resort. There was no hint of a military base (i.e., Camp Humphreys) on the map.

Sandy had brought a dictionary/phrase book with her, but it was strictly English-Korean. We wandered through the village square, trying to find someone who might speak English. I remembered the Korean word for English, *yongo,* but when we approached folks on the streets or in shops and said, "*Yongo hasseyo?*" they shook their heads with a shrug and turned away as if we were lepers. Perhaps it was because we were wearing shorts in the very hot weather, which was OK on base, but not acceptable in the countryside. Or perhaps it was because Koreans don't like to admit they don't know something or can't help, as that would create loss of face.

When we returned to the car after our futile efforts at communication, a small, elderly lady holding a package was standing next to it. She spoke to us in Korean. Sandy was hopeful and asked her (in English) if she knew the way to the army base. The woman pointed straight ahead. Then the woman opened the rear car door, stepped in and sat down in the back seat with her package. We were surprised. We imagined that she thought we were lost Americans wanting to find the military base, and she intended to show us the way. We got into the car, and I drove straight ahead.

We rode for a while, and I began to worry because we were low on gas. When I saw a gas station, I pulled in and gave the attendant some Korean money (*won*, ₩) and asked if he spoke English. He, too, shook his head but filled the tank, which cost a good deal more than it would have on base. He gave us a box of Korean style tissues and some wrapped candy, apparently a bonus for the fill-up. The lady sat silently in the back seat of the car.

When we drove back onto the road, she pointed straight ahead again. Every once in a while, she uttered something guttural and, when she did, I would slow down. She then waved her hand, indicating straight ahead. We came to another village—just a collection of houses—and she became more voluble, jabbering and waving her hands. I slowed down, but she continued to wave forward. After we passed through the village, she said something and pointed right. The only landmark was a dirt turn-out. I pulled over and stopped the car. She got out with her package, smiled, and bowed. We realized we had just driven her home.

Korea, Are You at Peace?

At that point we were—more than just figuratively—pretty far off base. I turned the car around and started back the way we had come. On the left, I noticed a symbol that seemed familiar. During one of our orientation trips, the director of the UMUC Korean Division had mentioned that a certain symbol—rather like a plate with fire in it—indicated a hotel. So I pulled in, hoping someone there might speak English. We went to the desk and tried communicating with words and hand gestures. The fellow at the desk didn't turn his back on us, as had the villagers. Perhaps he thought we were potential customers. Unfortunately, he also didn't understand us.

Finally, Sandy said something about "army" and he perked up. "Ah, almee."

"Yes, yes," we both declared, grinning.

He pulled out a piece of paper and started drawing a map. He began the map with a road framed by two lines, rather widely separated. Since he had started it in the middle of the paper, he ran out of paper before he had gotten very far with the map. All of the Y-forks and X-intersections were also doubled-lined of course. So, he crumpled up the first map and started his new map near the bottom of a clean page, but again ran out of space on the page and became frustrated.

Then he had a better idea. He took us to the second floor of the hotel, stepped out onto a balcony, and pointed off to the left. We could see a Purina-Chow checkerboard pattern painted on a water tower. As he pointed, he said, "Almee." We realized that we could use that water tower as our beacon. We both knew the Korean phrase for "Thank you" (*Kam-sa-ham-nida*), and we thanked him profusely, bowing. He bowed back, and we went on our way.

We drove back onto the road and turned left toward the water tower as soon as we could. But wide fields lay between us and the water tower. Soon we couldn't see the tower behind some trees. When we passed the trees, the water tower was behind us, so we turned left again. We kept zigzagging, turning in the direction of the water tower whenever we could see it. Eventually, I saw a familiar road and realized that it was the same *wrong* road we had taken initially, so I turned around and, in about a mile, we saw a four lane boulevard off to our left.

I turned to Sandy and asked, "Does this look like the kind of wide, well paved road that might lead to a military installation?"

Sandy said, "We can try it."

We turned onto it, and in about half a mile we arrived at Camp Humphreys. I was glad we had gotten gas.

Our meanderings had consumed an hour and a half, and darkness was about to descend. We went into the Base Exchange and asked the man at the information desk, a Korean, how to return to Osan. He drew a map, again with the double-lined roads, throwing away the map after running out of paper, until he finally produced a satisfactory one. He warned us that most Americans get lost on the way back to Osan by missing a left turn into what seems like wilderness. Instead, they go straight into the town of Songtan, which surrounds the base on three sides.

We had no trouble with the drive back until we were almost at the base, and by that time it was dark. When I began to see lights and shops, I realized we had missed the elusive left turn and stopped the car.

Sandy said, "What are you doing?"

I tried to explain. "I don't recognize this. I think we're going into town. I'm turning around."

So I did a U-turn and took the first right turn (the missed left) onto a backcountry road. Sandy's voice was strained when she asked, "Where are you going?"

"I think this is our road," I replied.

She sat silently as we drove through the dark countryside. When barbed wire appeared on the left, she became relieved.

Korea, Are You at Peace?

Soon, I recognized a newly constructed—and already disintegrating—apartment building, its siding shredding, just outside the back gate to Osan airbase. I said, "This is it, Sandy. We're here."

"Good going," she responded, exhaling noticeably.

Initial anxieties about going into the Korean community by myself began to give way to a sense that I could cope with almost anything. I had learned the Korean alphabet (*Hangul*) shortly after arriving, and I was soon able to read signs on shops and public buildings. I was surprised and pleased to be able to decipher a place name or a familiar English cognate—such as *kop'e* which means coffee.

Subsequently, I took several trips by car into the countryside, either alone or with other faculty members. We had to put new brake pads and a master cylinder in it, as well as bushings on one of the front wheels, and we changed the oil and air filters. The engine ran very well. The work and parts were reasonable, but repairs involved going out into the local economy with a little help from others who had been there before.

Driving on Korean roads and highways always felt hazardous; Koreans drive as fast as they can, wherever they are. The most threatening vehicles on the roads are buses. Buses dominate traffic and have a lane to themselves on super-highways like the Kyongbu Expressway, the main north-south expressway that runs down the center of the country from Seoul to Pusan. Only the boldest Korean drivers, with the fastest and most responsive cars, dare enter the bus lane for fear they will not be able to vacate it quickly enough to get out of the way of a bus barreling down upon them.

A Korean bus driver once tried to run down my car because I was not going fast enough on the streets of Pyongt'aek, the town near Camp Humphreys. When I slowed to let an old lady cross the street, he honked his horn and blinked his lights behind my car.

Then another driver saw a chance to do a U-turn as my car slowed down, and I had to put on the brakes. This further enraged the bus driver, who continued to honk his horn and flash his lights all the way to Camp Humphreys. At a stoplight just outside the base, the bus pulled to my right, and the driver turned around and glowered at me. I put my hand on the roof and raised two fingers in a victory sign and then lowered the index finger. He became enraged, got out of his bus, came around to the open window of my car, and started yelling at me in Korean.

I said calmly, in English, "There was a lady crossing the street."

He was practically apoplectic and gave me the finger twice. I feigned ignorance. When the light changed, I drove ahead into Camp Humphries. Sandy was appalled when she realized what I had done. I felt some remorse but didn't think I had created a serious international incident. Still, resentment of foreigners in one's land grows from many such small insults and misunderstandings.

THE CAR, apartment building, Songtan

Chapter 3

THREE FOREIGN CULTURES

It soon became clear that I was interfacing with not just one "foreign culture" in Korea but three. First, I operated within the UMUC Overseas program, which was unlike any academic environment I'd known before. Second, I had to navigate the Korean culture, influenced by an American military presence on nearby bases. Third, and perhaps most daunting, was the challenge of maneuvering through the rigid and seemingly capricious regulations of the American military apparatus. Each of these three cultures had its own rules and assumptions, and many were unwritten and unexamined.

By contrast, Isabella Bishop, a minister's daughter, interacted primarily with missionaries and missionary organizations in place when she arrived in Korea. These were the havens from which she prepared to sally forth into the countryside on her own. In Pusan, she contacted three Australian missionaries with whom she lodged while there. She admired their pluck in living with the native population and their concern for the lives of the locals, and she recommended their behavior as an effective missionary method. Local contacts throughout her time in this part of the world came largely through missionaries on the scene.

As a British citizen, she also had ready access to the foreign diplomatic corps while staying in major Korean cities—primarily the British Consulate and contacts afforded by them. But during her long forays into the countryside, she was largely on her own and face-to-face with Korean people in their local villages. Sometimes she felt mobbed and overwhelmed. She was the first Western woman—in most cases the first Westerner—that any rural Koreans had seen, and she was an object of intense curiosity to the peasantry. She passed off this often aggressive curiosity with amused tolerance. But she became increasingly annoyed and extremely disdainful of the upper class (*yangban*) administrators who appeared only to serve their own interests while oppressing the peasants in their jurisdiction.

The yangban comprised the hereditary upper class of Yi-dynasty Korea, perhaps the most rigidly hierarchical society in East Asia at the time. Yangban men were trained as Confucian scholars and held all official positions in the central government and in the countryside. By the nineteenth century, they had become social parasites rather than public servants. Whenever Isabella Bishop was forced to deal with these officials, her ire was aroused and she pulled no punches expressing it.

> *"For among the curses of Korea is the existence of this privileged class of yang-bans or nobles, who must not work for their own living... A yang-ban carries nothing for himself, not even his pipe... He is supported on his led horse, and supreme helplessness is the conventional requirement... His servants browbeat and bully the people, and take fowls and eggs without payment..."*[9]

Hence, differences in our Korean experiences reflected not only the enormous political shifts of the intervening century, but also the biases of our support groups. Our views of the country were similarly colored by another cultural lens: we each held citizenship in a world-dominating culture that allowed women substantial freedom. Bishop was raised in a highly religious nineteenth century family and had become a famous travel writer. I was trained as an academic biomedical scientist and traveled mostly for the pleasure of exploring unknown cultures.

One unexpectedly foreign culture in which I became embedded was the academic environment of the University of Maryland, Overseas. UMUC serves at the pleasure and expense of the military and tries to please that boss while attempting to maintain the academic standards of a stateside institution with a solid reputation. When I was there, the administrative staff consisted primarily of American expatriates who wished to retain American citizenship and perks while living outside the U.S. Many began as faculty members and then chose to stay in Asia for varying reasons, often involving a spouse—an American spouse they were trying to get away from or an Asian spouse they had acquired. Assisting the administrators were Koreans with excellent English proficiency. These assistants were able to negotiate with local individuals, businesses, and the government bureaucracy.

The UMUC faculty consisted of an odd assortment of adventurers and misfits, with a few military spouses and some Koreans in the mix. Most were Americans with some story, such as bucking the tenure system at a more traditional institution and then leaving in frustration. The quirky mindset of many of the faculty could be inferred from their child-naming habits. At a small gathering of faculty at Osan, Daniel, a physicist, was there with his Korean wife and their year-old daughter, Galaxy. The issue of children's names came up, and I realized that all the children there had fanciful names, like Aurora or Prima, reflecting the whimsically independent character of their faculty parents.

A few Korean students enrolled in my biology classes—ROK soldiers, base contractors, wives or college-age dependents of military personnel. The Koreans either did very well in class or dropped out early. They were usually studious and conscientious despite the difficulty of learning the exotic language of biology embedded in English, another foreign language.

Indeed, one of my best students that first year was a ROK soldier at Camp Humphreys, who took fastidious notes and came up to me every evening after class, asking me to fill in his blanks with words—both ordinary English words and biological terminology—that he hadn't understood during the lecture. Usually we could figure out what was missing. But sometimes I didn't remember what I had said at that particular moment and would paraphrase the idea for him. This he dutifully took down in the margins of his notebook. He was the top-scoring student in class that term.

Several Koreans also worked with UMUC; I established good rapport with a few, although we were all so busy doing our jobs that we rarely had time for socializing. One wonderful and helpful Korean woman was a logistics person for UMUC in Seoul. She arranged housing, directed me to local resources, and had the skill and charm to solve such diverse problems as obtaining biological specimens for use in lab experiments and securing military billeting for me in Taegu when the heater in my apartment became non-functional during a record cold snap.

One of the secretaries at the UMUC office in Osan AFB was a lively Korean woman married to a retired American serviceman who worked at the base auto shop. She was always enthusiastic, knew the base thoroughly, and was willing to walk me to those places I needed to go to solve bureaucratic problems. She helped with early difficulties in obtaining a ration control card, for shopping at the commissary, and in acquiring a SOFA stamp in my passport, necessary for traveling outside Korea.

SOFA, an acronym for Status of Forces Agreement, means that the American Armed Forces have legal jurisdiction over any U.S. military personnel and contractors in the foreign country. Thus, Americans in the service of the military are outside the law of the country in which they are living and working. This occasionally causes local outrage, especially if an egregious crime is committed by a military person outside a military base. I learned what SOFA meant only after returning to the U.S. I was never able to find someone in the UMUC office to decipher the acronym for me or tell me why it was so important.

During my daily life off-base (on the economy), I interacted mostly with Koreans. I shopped in local markets, walked to and from base through Korean streets lined by Korean shops and homes, and sometimes ate at local restaurants. In my travels around the countryside as a solitary tourist—or going from base to base by bus or train for teaching—I encountered many groups of Korean tourists.

Korean tourist groups were usually good humored and intense. They reminded me of some American tourist groups—loud, aggressive, and indifferent to others around them. One notable difference was that Korean tourists often voluntarily segregated themselves by gender, men clustering in one group and women in another. This separation was so marked that if a group was very large, one bus might hold women and another, men. Then at a travel stop, they would get together and mingle in the restaurant. I could only assume that this segregation was preferred by everyone involved.

In groups, Korean men were generally boisterous and noisy, especially after drinking *soju*, the national alcoholic beverage—much like vodka with a bit more flavor. Drinking seemed to begin after work in the afternoon or evening.

Koreans are generally practical people, more concerned with

function than appearance, except in matters of clothing and cars. And they seemed always in a hurry. *Pali. Pali,* means 'Let's go, let's go.' or 'Hurry, hurry.' It's a stock phrase urged by Korean mothers upon their children, who dutifully internalize it.

Another faculty member in Osan had spent nine years in Italy and claimed that Koreans were much like Italians. Certainly they drove like Italians, zipping in and out of traffic lanes and up onto sidewalks to get ahead of whatever traffic was clogging the way to their destination. And they left cars parked on any vacant roadside shoulder or sidewalk, although sidewalks were scarce except alongside major city streets.

Korean children were almost always delightful—attractive, curious and unabashed. Adults were sometimes friendly and welcoming and sometimes inconsiderate. In my experience, men and women exhibited great differences in behavioral styles. Men were more likely to be rude than women. Women were usually open and smilingly helpful; otherwise they would simply ignore my question rather than giving me a sneer or a rough answer. Women, probably because of their traditional second-class status, tended to be supportive and friendly with one another and even toward me, a foreign woman.

Eventually, I came to know several Korean women and developed friendships with a couple of them. By contrast, I made friends with only one Korean man, a UMUC faculty member who lived part-time in the U.S. where he had family, and part-time in Korea when he taught there. Another young man I met on a plane was very helpful on an arrival at Kimpo airport in Seoul, and I maintained some contact with him and his wife while in Korea.

The culture I penetrated the least was the military, although it surrounded me whenever I taught or went on base to shop. UMUC Overseas Division is like a social symbiont of the military. Whereas Koreans I met esteemed teachers and treated them with great respect, military personnel, particularly the upper echelon, tended to view UMUC faculty members as financially dependent contractors of virtually servant status.

My main contact with military personnel was during class time. This was a pretty uneven exchange; students were there primarily to hear me speak, not *vice versa*, and initially I didn't get a very good sense of what their lives were like. This changed after I had been in country a few months, came to know several soldiers, and heard many life stories.

Some students told stories of unhappy childhoods in deprived or abusive conditions, and I gained a great appreciation for the military as a source of structure and guidance for directionless youth, as a social safety net, and as an institution that provides both career and personal opportunity for many who might otherwise not have access to such resources.

By and large, military personnel were in classes to gain credentials for stateside jobs after they retired, usually around age forty. A biology course simply fulfilled a science requirement for a degree in a more practical area such as accounting or business administration. Thus, students were motivated to pass the class but not necessarily to excel, although several did. Servicemen sometimes complained of being bored, and their motivation for taking classes may sometimes have been simply to do something with their time. Most, though, were in class to get a degree so they would be able to find a good job after leaving the service.

Such readily available, inexpensive college education and on-the-job skill training are valuable perks of a career in the military. Most of those in my classes were career servicemen. Often I had students from the Intelligence Division in class. Some, the linguists, were able to speak Korean and tended to do well in the biology courses. They were smart, and I'm sure they did well in all their courses. Other soldiers had a tougher time of it. Only one of the military students in my classes eventually majored in biology. He was a linguist married to a Korean woman; he took several biology classes; and he was a consistently excellent student.

I spent time on enough military bases to get a feel for the general policy of the American military overseas. Create a Little America and surround it with high fences and barbed concertina wire. Each military base has apartment complexes, a movie theater, various types of stores (usually at least a liquor store and a bookstore), a laundromat, a barber shop, a gas station, fast-food places (Wendy's, Chick-fil-A), and sometimes a car dealership. In addition, there is the Base Exchange (BX) or Post Exchange (PX), similar to a down-sized Wal-Mart and the commissary, roughly equivalent to a stateside supermarket. Thus a U.S. military base resembles Small Town, U.S.A. On many bases, an elementary school and a high school provide education to children of military families; these schools are staffed with very well-paid civilian teachers. Those I knew earned more than the UMUC college faculty.

One can live an entire tour of duty on base. One of my students, in fact, did just that. At the end of a class term, when he was about to rotate back to the States after two years in Korea, he confessed to me that he had never gone off an American military installation. He had taken military buses from base to base (Osan to Yongsan), as well as to Kimpo Airport in Seoul. But he had stayed—whenever and wherever possible—within the confines of familiar buildings, social structures, symbols and language.

Of the three cultures that formed the maze of my daily life in Korea, the one I became most familiar with and could maneuver with the greatest ease was the UMUC academic environment. Colleagues and administrators were supportive, and most understood the difficulties involved in trying to offer quality learning in an unfamiliar environment with scarce resources.

The Korean culture eventually became increasingly familiar through constant interactions on the street and through reading and traveling around the country. I took an Asian history course taught on base by UMUC; this was enormously helpful to my understanding of Asian culture in general and of Korean culture in particular. The teacher was a Korean who had spent several years in the U.S. and knew both cultures well.

I tried learning the Korean language but with limited success. Nonetheless, I did learn the alphabet, which is phonetic and fairly easy to learn; I also learned the structure of syllables, and a bit of grammar. My minimal Korean was enough to prompt a taxi driver try to engage me in rapid-fire conversation, to which I couldn't respond. Nonetheless, this admittedly meager language skill allowed me to explore the countryside on my own with little trepidation. I learned early on to bring a dictionary everywhere.

I came to know a few Korean women reasonably well, as one might a neighbor with whom one chats over the fence a couple times a week. The language barrier prevented any deep personal knowledge, although I occasionally glimpsed inner lives through wistful glances and expressive hand gestures.

It was not easy to develop strategies for navigating the three cultures through which my daily life threaded—academic, Korean, and military. At first the challenge was exciting, and then frustrations began to feel overwhelming. Finally, familiarity brought back a sense of peace.

Colorful painted eaves on Buddhist temple

Chapter 4

THE DEMILITARIZED ZONE (DMZ)

After about a month in Korea I had almost settled in. At this point, everyday annoyances no longer felt like challenges to be overcome, but rather aggravations, because I knew I would be dealing with them indefinitely. The fun of trying to solve problems or mediate hassles had faded. I regretted moving beyond the wide-eyed adventurer phase of discovery. The time-requiring business of doing the job I was hired to do—teaching biology to American military students on bases—consumed me utterly. I had hit the ground running on arriving at Osan AFB. The second huge time-drain was the business of simply living: setting up an apartment off base, buying household items (sheets, towels, dishes), buying groceries, and finding my way around the airbase and the town of Songtan.

At one point I felt really stressed, as if my life were one large mat of loose ends. Teaching duties threatened to get ahead of me: grading papers and tests, reading the text, and preparing class lectures. I was forced to make up a three-hour class because the high school where we held many evening classes had canceled university classes with just one day's notice. I had not been able to get online for six days, because the computer lab was closed for the Korean holiday of *Chusok*, a harvest celebration. Chusok is probably the major Korean holiday, a time devoted to family and festivities. It's comparable to the extensive, weeks-long celebration of Western Christmas.

Indeed, at Osan AFB we celebrated any and all holidays—American and Korean. Most base workers were Koreans, and their bosses were Americans. This meant that buildings and services might be closed unexpectedly, apparently randomly. For example, since Labor Day was on a Monday, but the commissary was normally closed on Mondays, it was also closed that Tuesday for a make-up day even though it had already been closed for the full four-day weekend.

And I had no luck making arrangements for a trip during the break between classes. I had wanted to go somewhere interesting—Thailand or China—during the three week interval between first and second terms. Somehow, all trips available through the base travel office were filled or weren't running, and I didn't have the confidence to make arrangements off-base.

Moreover, my temporary ration control card, which had to be shown every time I bought groceries at the commissary, was due to expire for the second time, and the permanent card was somewhere in the pipeline, but nobody knew where, nor when it would arrive. Then I discovered that my electricity bill was overdue, and I couldn't pay it at the bank if it was overdue, a detail of living on the economy that had somehow slipped through the instructional cracks during orientation.

But near the end of that week, things began to weave themselves together. I finally received the permanent ration control card. I passed the test for a SOFA driver's license. I eventually found the Korean Electric Power Company—with the help of a map drawn by a Korean shop keeper—and paid the overdue bill. An envelope of mail that my daughter had sent from home in mid-August to Yokota (the UMUC main Asian office in Japan) finally arrived in Osan in late September. So I got caught up on my American financial status and paid old bills. Also, a trip to Thailand was shaping up for the break between classes. It all required faith, hope, charity and a dogged persistence.

One place I really wanted to see in Korea was the Korean Demilitarized Zone, the DMZ—a four-kilometer (2.5 mile) wide, 250-kilometer (155 miles) long gash that snakes across the Korean peninsula at roughly the 38th parallel. This forbidding, uninhabited stretch of land between the two Koreas symbolizes a wound that continues to fester in the Korean psyche, a forced division of a country that had long been culturally and linguistically unified. The division has separated relatives and compatriots across a politically arbitrary divide for the past half century. It is a living reminder of the Korean War, a war that began as a tragic miscalculation and has not yet ended.[10] The DMZ symbolizes the national helplessness experienced by a small country in the face of the military might of world powers seeking to control its fate. Although military personnel and their families were given priority for this excursion, after several requests I was finally put on the list to visit the DMZ.

When Westerners speak of Korea, we normally mean South Korea. When referring to the northern part of the peninsula, we use the term North Korea, a very different country, currently inaccessible and more-or-less threatening. When Isabella Bishop visited Korea slightly more than a century ago, it included the entire peninsula from Manchuria in the north-west to the island of Chejudo off its southern coast. During the century-long interval between our travels, Korea was wrenched from its traditional culture and preferred isolation by devastating wars and occupations. Ultimately, South Korea underwent a prolonged and violent transition from a traditional Confucian culture to a thriving, modern, technological nation whose current economic success places it among Asia's four Little Tigers. By contrast, North Korea is now a contemporary version of the medieval country Isabella Bishop witnessed, with its posturing pomp and ceremony, and its hierarchical, paternalistic culture. Since 1948, the communist DPRK and its citizens remain trapped in an absolutist cultural vision that will never materialize.

Thus, the Korean peninsula has become a contemporary political tinderbox, with North Korea—a nuclear nation—viewing South Korea as its legitimate territory. These two utterly contrasting countries are divided by the DMZ.

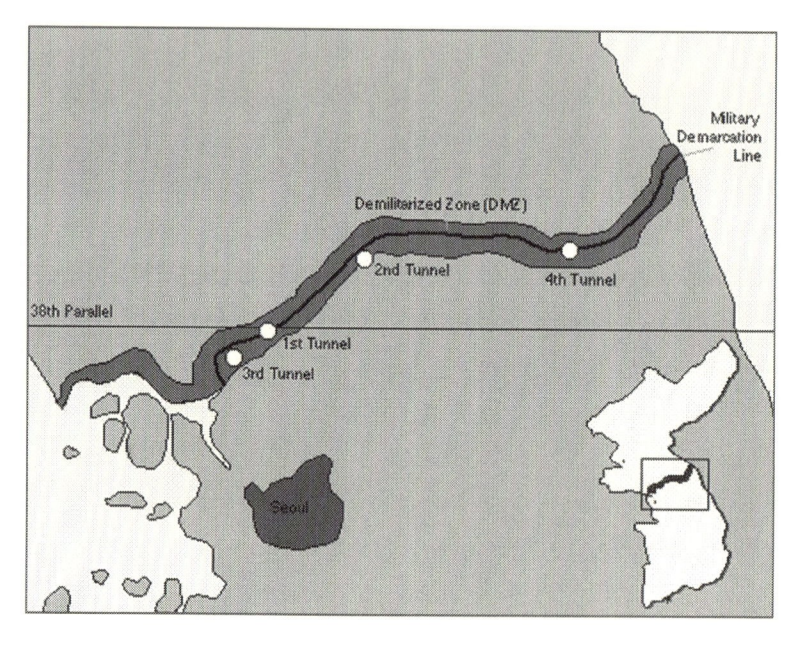

The DMZ stretches across the Korean peninsula.[11]

How did this division come about in a once-united, ethnically homogeneous country? It is a long, sad, convoluted tale of military posturing, ideological intransigence, and political ambition. The seeds of this debacle were sown while Isabella Bishop was still in Korea, when the Korean Queen Min was murdered with the complicity of the Japanese, and the Russian embassy in Korea subsequently sheltered King Kojong against assassination. The dissonance was amplified by competing Japanese and Russian military ambitions in East Asia, both vying for hegemony over Korea after the Japanese defeated Chinese troops on Korean soil in 1895. Japan and Russia considered dividing Korea into two "spheres of influence" along the 38th parallel in a proposed agreement that never went into effect. However, Japan won the ensuing Russo-Japanese war (1904 – '05), temporarily ending any Russian claims in Korea. Japanese annexation of Korea (1910 – '45) was the first step in its imperialistic expansion throughout East Asia. A synopsis of Korean history is offered in the Appendix.

At the end of World War II in 1945, Korea was again up for grabs. As the war with Japan drew to a close, Russia (the USSR) began sending troops from Manchuria into northern Korea. Concerned that the whole peninsula would be overrun by Communists, American military officers, Dean Rusk and Charles Bonesteel, urged that the 38th parallel become the line of demarcation between occupying Soviet and Allied troops. The Soviets complied.

It took three years for some semblance of stability to return to the devastated Korean landscape, but in August and September of 1948, the U.S.-backed Republic of Korea (ROK) and the Soviet-backed Democratic People's Republic of Korea (DPRK) were proclaimed independent countries, south and north of the 38th parallel respectively. Each of the "independent" countries thus formed implicitly believed that the whole peninsula should be included within its jurisdiction. Within a year, Soviet and U.S. forces departed.

But that was far from the end of the story. In June, 1950 North Korea (with Soviet and Chinese backing) invaded South Korea and overran the capital, Seoul. It was a blitzkrieg. The U.S. became alarmed and mobilized U.N. troops stationed in Japan in an effort to repulse the invasion. The army invading from the North was only halted at the Pusan Perimeter, a line of military encampments hastily constructed in the south-eastern region of the country and staunchly defended under General MacArthur's command. In September of that year, MacArthur launched the successful Inchon offensive, cutting off the bulk of the North Korean troops and recapturing Seoul. His troops then pressed north, crossed the 38th parallel, and captured Pyongyang, the DPRK capital.

At this point, the Chinese felt threatened. They sent in troops that had earlier amassed at the North Korean border and began driving U.N. troops south again, all the way to Suwon and Wonju, south of Seoul. In the spring of 1951, U.N. troops once again pressed north, recaptured Seoul, and crossed the 38th parallel deep into communist territory, all the way to the border with China. The Chinese persuaded the USSR to send in air cover, which once again turned the momentum of war southward. This bitter and destructive struggle lasted another two years, with neither side gaining significant advantage, but with enormous loss of life, both military and civilian. The population of both North and South Korea was decimated.[12] Moreover, the destruction of dwellings and vegetation utterly devastated a country already impoverished by a half-century of Japanese occupation.

The Korean conflict is considered by many to be the first battle of the world-wide, half-century-long Cold War. The relentless destruction of life and resources in this conflict is chillingly chronicled by David Halberstam in *The Coldest Winter*.[13]

Ultimately, an armistice agreement was signed in 1953, resulting in the cessation of hostilities and establishment of the Korean DMZ, which separated the two hostile nations by a no-man's land between them. This was just a truce however, not a peace treaty, and the two countries are still technically at war. Since that time, North and South Korea have gone their separate ways politically and economically, each aware of the potential threat of the other and always intending, however fancifully, to re-unite the peninsula and subsume the other Korea into its own political structure.

In more than half a century since the armistice, many attempts at rapprochement have been initiated—sometimes by the South and sometimes by the North. Most often, those efforts came down to political posturing. The North Korean dictatorship under Kim Il-sung, and later under his son, Kim Jong-il, has been intransigent in asserting that the whole Korean peninsula be included in their regime. The grandson, Kim Jong-un is currently spouting even more belligerent rhetoric than his forebears. He has taken a highly aggressive tone and has threatened nuclear attack on the South and its "evil occupiers," the United States.

During the East-West thaw in the late 1980 and early '90s, when Russia recognized South Korea's statehood and established diplomatic relations with Seoul, Kim Il Sung became concerned for the survival of his country and his regime. He threatened to develop nuclear weapons, which the Soviet Union had always opposed. A North Korean nuclear program developed slowly, with aid from Pakistan, but was eventually successful. Pyongyang withdrew from the Nuclear Non-Proliferation treaty in 2003, and conducted its first underground nuclear test in 2006, as confirmed by seismic records. Many other hostile acts on the part of North Korea (terrorist bombings, assassinations) have occurred since the DMZ was established. Despite occasional expressions of good will from one side or the other, the two halves of the peninsula are now almost irrevocably separate and hostile countries.

After two months in Korea, I visited the DMZ on a week-end bus trip organized by the military at Osan AFB. I wanted to witness and understand this tragic symbol of Korean history, this metaphor of a unique political and cultural schizophrenia. Until the DMZ trip, I hadn't much reflected on the political stalemate and military time bomb still threatening the Korean peninsula. The village of Panmunjom, within the thin strip of land that constitutes the DMZ, is where the truce was signed, terminating the vicious three year

Korean War (1950 – '53). The U.N. troops at Panmunjom are always on high alert, and the tension in the air was almost palpable.

On opposite sides of the DML—a "demilitarized line" about the width of a football field separating the hostile factions—are towers about three or four stories high. In them, soldiers peer through binoculars at each other and at the intrepid tourists who venture into the site. I didn't see any tourists on the northern side of the DML. Soldiers from both sides—on the ground and in the towers—glare across the distance, daring each other to make a suspicious move. South Korean soldiers adopt a *taekwondo* stance, fists at their sides, knees bent, shoulders hunched—as if crouching animals prepared to strike—a posture intended to intimidate the North Koreans.

In the U.N. area was a tower constructed with a Korean Buddhist temple motif—colorful roof tiles and graceful wall paintings. This building contrasted brightly with the otherwise squat and somber bunker-like architecture of its surroundings and with the gray reality of a half-century-long stand-off between the old familiar enemies on opposite sides of the fence. We went into the room where the temporary truce had been signed in 1953. Our guide, an American soldier stationed at the DMZ, emphasized that what exists between North Korea and South Korea is an armistice, not a peace treaty, and that the countries are still officially at war. That was a sobering realization.

The North Koreans have dug several tunnels beneath the DMZ into South Korea. Four tunnels had been discovered when I was there. Another twenty were rumored to exist. We were allowed to visit one of the tunnels.

Along with eight others in the group, I descended slowly into the bowel of the tunnel. Its dirt walls and muddy steps were slippery, but a railing made the descent manageable. The lower part of the tunnel was dank and dark, and we didn't stay long. The trek back up the tunnel steps was both treacherous and exhausting, especially for me, as I was far from military fitness. I'm sure that soldiers passing through the tunnel would be in much better shape. Nonetheless, with its narrow width, steep grade, and uneven terrain, the tunnel would certainly not be an efficient way to get soldiers from North to South. I seriously doubt it would be a route for surprise military attack. More likely, these passageways were for spies. Still, the mere existence of tunnels beneath the DMZ has generated a fear factor for South Koreans.

A few soldiers and a civilian have been killed in incidents at the DMZ. One in 1976 was the bludgeoning deaths of two American soldiers by North Koreans over an effort to trim a poplar tree. This nearly led to an all-out military confrontation between the U.S. and North Korea.

On the southern edge of the DMZ is a concrete wall—the Korean Wall—built by the South and intended as an anti-tank barrier. Along the northern border of the DMZ is a heavily electrified (3kV) triple fence, built by the North. And the land between them is strewn with mines.

A small, positive consequence of this no-man's land is that a thin swath across the Korean peninsula near the 38th parallel has become a *de facto* wildlife sanctuary, teeming with birds, including a large flock of Manchurian cranes, small mammals, and even some endangered larger animals such as the Asiatic black bear. Indeed, some of the flora and fauna found there may no longer exist elsewhere on the Korean peninsula. Environmentalists everywhere hope that, if the country is reunited, the DMZ will remain uninhabited by humans. At present, an international effort is underway by the DMZ Forum, an ecologic advocacy group, to preserve this once-grim symbol of war as a monument to peace and preservation.

Tunnel entrance, DMZ

SECTION II:

Into The Korean Backcountry

Overcoming initial difficulties with language and customs, Isabella and I each found means of traveling away from Korea's cities, which we both found particularly noisome, into the beautiful countryside. We both marveled at the exquisite scenery in a land of gentle mountains and rivers uncorrupted by the environmentally corrosive Western culture from which we had come. During our backcountry adventures, we each experienced difficulties with transportation—she by sampan and pony; I by car, bus and train. We also both suffered the hazards of heavy monsoon rains. Moreover, Bishop was forced to divert her itinerary because of an impending war between Japan and China on Korean soil.

Chapter 5

OUT OF TOWN AND INTO THE MOUNTAINS

Isabella Bishop spent weeks in Seoul trying to gather supplies, servants, and most importantly, a reliable translator, for her three month foray into the country's interior. Problems finding a translator were eventually solved by a young missionary, Mr. Miller, who was still perfecting his grasp of the language. He brought along his Korean servant, Che-on-I, and the two of them together were able to function as able translators. Mr. Wong, a Chinese cook and general factotum, was also a constant help to her during the trip. Most of the journey was accomplished by *sampan*, a shallow-bottomed boat with a small cabin for protection and some privacy.

Besides herself, a crew of two Korean boatmen, and the three helpers listed above, she loaded into the sampan the minimum necessities of life. These included food (*e.g.*, live chickens), cooking utensils, clothing, sleeping mats, and a great deal of Korean money, which she called "cash." This cash consisted of heavy copper coins not worth much in single denominations; she viewed it largely as ballast. She also brought along two cameras, photographic plates, and developing materials, with which she obtained some of the earliest photographs of Korea. Several of these illustrate *Korea and her Neighbors*.[14] One of the first is a picture of her sampan on the

Han River, which I had seen reprinted in Jon Carter Covell's *Korea's Cultural Roots*.[15]

Thus, Isabella Bird Bishop set out on the first leg of her independent adventure in a twenty-eight by four foot sampan—one woman and five men—up the Han River and its branches into the wild and unexplored backcountry of *Choson*, 'land of morning calm.' She found the scenery along the Han River (*Han-gang*) enchanting.

> "[T]he scenery varied hourly, and after the first few days became not only beautiful, but in places magnificent, and full of surprises; the spring was in its early beauty, and the trees in their first vividness of green, red, and gold; the flowers and flowering shrubs were in their glory, the crops at their most attractive stage, birds sang in the thickets, rich fragrant odors were wafted off the water...and the waters of the Han were clear as crystal..."[16]
>
> After circumventing the fine fortress summit of Nam Han, the river enters the mountains. From that time up to the head of possible navigation, the scenery in its variety, beauty and unexpectedness exhausts the vocabulary of admiration."[17]

The countryside was alive with wild birds, including cranes, egrets and pink ibis. She also wrote that leopards, antelopes and Korean tigers were found among the mountains along the Han. She was initially suspicious of reports of tigers, suspecting that damage to livestock and human life, presumably caused by tigers, was really the work of leopards. These big cats were often seen in villages, and sometimes even in the city of Seoul.

Isabella Bishop and her crew were forced to ascend rapids along the south fork of the Han River and to negotiate with villagers along the way for supplies, both of which were difficult although not dangerous. She described Korean village peasants as friendly but annoyingly curious, especially the women. During one village stay she was virtually assaulted in the women's quarters.

> "I was laid hold of (literally) by the serving women and dragged through the women's court and into the women's apartment. I was surrounded by fully forty women. . .They investigated my clothing, pulled me about, took off my hat and tried it on, untwisted my hair and absorbed my hairpins, pulled off my gloves and tried them on with shrieks of laughter. . ."[18]

After departing Seoul, the first town of any importance she came to was Yo-Ju. The town centered on a *yamen*, the official government building and administrative center of the region. All the officials were yangban, hereditary upper-class administrators and scholars. Her distaste for Korean officialdom and of the yangban upper class is obvious from her description of experiences there; other expressions of disgust and annoyance for these "social parasites" recur throughout her book. In the yamens to which she paid obligatory visits if passing through their district, she found officials lounging about, pretending to govern. In her view, their activity was purposeless, except that they took whatever they wished (justified as tax) from local peasants and from travelers who happened to pass through the area.

> "[W]ithin the gates [of the yamen] were plenty of those persons who suck the lifeblood of Korea. There were soldiers with Tyrolese hats and coarse cotton uniforms in which blue predominated, yamen runners in abundance, writers, officers of **in**justice [the **in** was italicized by I.B.], messengers pretending to have business on hand and. . .many more men sitting on the floor smoking long pipes. . ."[19]

Upon leaving Yo-Ju, the river narrowed, and rapids became increasingly steep and treacherous. Her destination was Soraksan, a revered mountain cluster in the eastern part of the country. Because of the rapids, her party was only able to navigate within sight of Sol-rak-san (as she transliterated the name), but they could not access the mountains by sampan. In late spring, the countryside was greening and picturesque. Azaleas and wisteria were in blossom, culminating in a magnificent river scene at To-tam.

> "[T]he beauty of the Han culminates at To-tam in the finest river view I had then ever seen, a broad stretch, with a deep bay and lofty limestone cliffs, between which, on a green slope, the picturesque, deep-eaved, brown-roofed houses of the village are built.. . . Guarding the entrance of the bay are three picturesque jagged pyramidal rocks...To the southwest, the Han, dark and deep, rolls out of sight around a pine-clad bluff among the magnificent ranges of the Sol-rak-San Mountains--masses of partially pine-clothed peaks and pinnacles of naked rock."[20]

Following the fall and winter terms teaching at local bases near Osan, I was assigned to teach a human biology course two evenings a week at Camp Long, a remote-site army base. For this assignment, I had to travel on my own into the Korean countryside. Camp Long is an American military base near Wonju, a town visited by Isabella Bishop during the first part of her travels into the Korean interior.

I obviously didn't travel from Songtan to Wonju by sampan that spring. Rather, I took a Korean intercity bus. On the many bus rides back and forth from Songtan to Wonju, I saw much of the same countryside as did Bishop during her river foray. I soon came to recognize special features of the countryside as distinctly Korean. Most notable were the mountains and the quaint Korean villages nestled in their foothills.

The Korean peninsula has been formed by mountains running from Manchuria southward to the Pacific. These form a spine along the eastern side of the peninsula, which splits about halfway down to form a less steep central chain. These old mountains, rather like the American Appalachians, have mellowed into gently jutting peaks and crags, only a few of which rise above the tree line. The eye is drawn down the mountainside to rice fields quilting the valleys below. And dotting many mountainsides are small mounds—hemispheres, perhaps two yards in diameter, covered with closely cropped grass. These are often grouped together around a stele of about the same height as the mounds. The steles are commemorative slabs of stone, engraved with text and sometimes with animal symbols. These were obviously family grave plots; usually no more than four or five mounds are clustered in one spot. These mounds lie on the steeper sections of the slopes. Obviously, Koreans didn't waste good bottom land for burial plots. Moreover, mountains are sacred in Korea, making them ideal sites for a final rest.

On one trip to Camp Long, I drove a rented car instead of taking the bus. It was the first leg of a week-long journey around the southeastern region of the country. This self-guided tour became possible because a military exercise was being held at Osan during a whole week in April. Classes there were canceled, to be rescheduled for some other time. I took advantage of the time off to travel into the Korean countryside on my own. However, classes were still held at Camp Long, so I went back there two evenings that week to teach.

By this time, I had learned the Korean alphabet and developed enough mastery of daily-usage words to be able to get by at bus stations, with taxi drivers, and with clerks at local *yogwans* (inexpensive Korean inns). I felt reasonably comfortable driving the throughway across the Korean peninsula on my own. Choosing not to risk the caprices of my dear (but not always roadworthy) Hyundai, I rented a new car at Osan airbase for the trip. I loaded the trunk with everything needed for the week—clothes, food, course materials, books about Korea, language books, and dictionaries—and headed into the backcountry.

I drove the throughway to Wonju, following the bus route I had taken so many times before. This time, I stopped at almost every rest area between Suwon and Wonju—sometimes to use the restaurant or rest-room, sometimes simply to experience the rest-stop culture. Besides indoor shops in a small strip mall offering amenities such as groceries, fast food and gifts, outdoor merchants hawked their wares from carts and trucks in the parking lot, giving rest stops a carnival atmosphere. At one stop, I picked up a map of Kangwondo Province that included a good, detailed map of Mount Sorak (Soraksan) and its vicinity.

Soraksan and the park bearing that name had been highly touted as the most beautiful mountains in the South by Koreans at both Osan and Camp Long. So I was determined to visit it. I initially thought that Soraksan was a single mountain, but in fact, it is a cluster of peaks, among the most revered sites on the Korean peninsula. It includes high, craggy mountains of the Taebaek mountain range, which forms a spine along the eastern side of the country. These are not quite as old as the gentler mountains running down the west-central part of the peninsula. But both ranges are beloved Korean mountains and provide a natural basis for the rock and mountain worship that lies at the heart of Korean folk customs. Indeed, rocks and mountains shape both the esthetic and the spiritual values of Koreans. Rocks decorate the fronts of buildings in cities and are integral to all Korean gardens—mostly large rocks sporting scant greenery and flowers. Soraksan is a huge natural garden of rocks, boulders, flowing water, and wild vegetation.

On the way to Soraksan, I drove eastward toward the East Sea. Koreans do *not* call the body of water between their country and Japan "The Sea of Japan," as it is labeled in most Western atlases. The

Korea, Are You at Peace?

Korean aversion to anything Japanese extends even to geographical names; hence Koreans call it *Tonghae* or East Sea. Korean officials mounted a campaign to establish this as the standard name in international cartography, citing centuries-old evidence. However, the argument was rejected in 2012 by the International Hydrographic Organization, the body governing names of bodies of water around the world.

Going eastward toward the sea, the throughway climbed steadily but not very steeply; tunnels cut through mountains eased the grade. The last rest stop before the coastal city of Kangnung was near a high hill with steps leading to a huge stele at the top. I decided to climb the hill despite a fierce wind coming out of the sea. The stele exhibited a standard motif for Korean monuments; the base was a turtle, and a tall, thin, rectangular slab rose from its back. Capping the slab was a black semicircle enclosing a pair of coiled dragons carved in *bas-relief*. In Eastern iconography, the turtle is a symbol of longevity and the dragon is a symbol of power. This combination is supposed to confer good luck and success on whatever lies nearby. According to David Mason (personal communication), these symbols can also be viewed as "...symbolic of the Trinity of Heaven, Earth and Humanity (*Cheon-Ji-In*), which is a fundamental room-concept of all oriental philosophy. Turtle symbolizes the Yin earth, dragons are the dynamic Yang powers of heaven [and] in between them is humanity, rectangular and standing, and that slab records what we accomplished between heaven and earth."

From the hilltop I could see the East Sea and the city of Kangnung at its edge. The road threading down, no longer a throughway, was forbiddingly steep and winding. After negotiating the descent, instead of going into Kangnung, I headed north toward Sokcho, expecting to find a place to stay in or near Soraksan National Park.

Soraksan is a sizable national park, still largely undefiled by commercial enterprises, where Koreans can enjoy the natural, craggy beauty of their eastern mountains. A sign directed me to a perimeter road surrounding the mountain cluster. On the drive around the park, the mountains and surroundings were largely deserted despite their fresh spring beauty. Bright yellow forsythia and pink azaleas punctuated nets of tree limbs budding in a thin haze of green and mauve. The weather was mild, and trees and bushes everywhere sported shades of white, yellow, and pink. The beginnings of leaves brushed dark branches with a delicate, wispy green of fresh, new growth. I stopped wherever I could find a pullout to view a fine scene of craggy boulders or a mountain panorama; this was not often. The scenery was awesome, but the road was very narrow. Korean roads seldom have full-width shoulders, even along throughways. Pulling off a winding road on a steep mountainside is dangerous under the best of circumstances and I feared it would be suicidal in Korea.

Few other cars were on the road; it almost seemed as if I had the park to myself. Springtime was a wonderful time to be there, although apparently not the tourist season. On my return, I was told that Koreans generally visited Soraksan either during the summer when they could enjoy nearby beaches or in the fall when leaves were most colorful.

As an American tourist, I expected to find lodging somewhere along the park's perimeter road. I had intended to stop in mid-afternoon and spend the next day exploring the park from there. However, I found no hotels, motels or yogwans. In fact, very few commercial enterprises existed along that road, and most of those I saw were closed. Along the entire perimeter drive, I found only one open tourist spot with a gift shop and restaurant. Most other park visitors, all Koreans, must have been in that shop as well. I left after buying a couple wooden items and some postcards. The limits of my Korean almost made the effort to buy postcards unsuccessful. The English-Korean dictionary I carried didn't include the term 'postcard.'

No overnight accommodations were evident on the perimeter drive, so I left the northeastern region of the park and drove toward the nearby coastal town of Sokcho. At an information kiosk near the edge of town, a kind woman tourist assistant gave me information and maps and directed me to a couple of reasonable hotels. She didn't speak much more English than I spoke Korean, but we eventually managed to communicate in a patient and pleasant way.

Korean women were almost universally helpful if it was in their power to be, particularly if they were approached with any sort of deference or grace. Their English, however, was usually spotty and difficult to understand. English is certainly as hard for Koreans to learn as Korean is for Americans, so communication required short words, hand gestures, pointing at maps, repetition and verification, interspersed with kind smiles, nods and deferential gestures.

I chose a hotel near the water and then took a long walk along the quays. Sokcho, a port town, didn't have much of a beach; fish shops and seafood restaurants lined most of the wharves and nearby back streets. I watched people cross a small inlet on a "people ferry," a wooden platform with rails on two sides. This was propelled by a ferry master pulling on ropes strung around pulleys attached to posts on both shores. He was helped by young boys who happened to be on the raft and who appeared to enjoy tugging on the thick ropes. I walked out to a lighthouse point, climbed to the top platform, and took photos of Sokcho from various heights.

I wanted to eat dinner but not in a fish restaurant, which was all I saw along the wharf. In one of the biology labs at Osan AFB, we had dissected fresh fish purchased at a local Songtan market; many of them contained parasites. The small, lively nematodes were an added attraction in the lab—fun for some students but horrifying to others. I believe we were all put off eating local fish after that experience. I went back to the car, got food from the supply in the trunk, and took it up to the hotel room, where I ate and read.

J. A. V. Simson

The main reading for this trip was a book by David Mason entitled *Spirit of the Mountains: Korea's San-shin and Traditions of Mountain Worship*.[21] This beautifully illustrated and fascinating treatment of Korean folk mountain culture enlightened and enlivened my appreciation for these and other Korean mountains.

Mason, an American expatriate from Michigan, lived and worked near Wonju. Intimately familiar with the Korean countryside, he also co-authored the 1997 edition of the *Lonely Planet Guide to Korea*. His *Spirit of the Mountains* focuses on Koreans' reverence for—and personification of—the mountains among which they live. It explores the pagan roots of mountain worship, and it illustrates imagery in which the mountain spirit (*San-shin*) has become interwoven with Buddhism and other religious traditions in Korea. Most San-shin images were photographed in Buddhist shrines in mountains and high places.

San-shin, the 'mountain spirit' or mountain god, was initially a shamanistic deity. The word 'shaman' is of Tungusic or eastern Siberian origin (the geographical source of the Korean language). It refers to the magic used to cure, divine, and control. Wherever a San-shin shrine or image is found, it represents a specific mountain or the surrounding mountain complex and is believed to protect nearby dwellings, humans, plants, and animals. This protection is extended to Buddhist monks, whose temple complexes are usually located in mountains, and to villagers living and farming in the valleys below. Images of San-shin were often found on inner walls of Buddhist temples or in ancillary buildings devoted to the deity. In researching his book, Mason collected over 500 photographs of sacred images (*San-shin-taeng-hwa*), several of which are included in the fine photographic reproductions that illuminate his book.

Mason analyzed these images for their iconographic content and found that they contained symbols of pre-Buddhist nature religion as well as Daoism and Buddhism. Although each image represents

Korea, Are You at Peace?

a specific mountain, most of them share iconic themes with other San-shin images. The major common characteristics include: a red robe clothing the deity, suggesting Chinese origin but representing kingship in Korea; the presence of a tiger, representing wilderness; and a pine tree near the figure, representing longevity. Indeed, Korean tigers were common in the mountains of that country until the 1930s.[22]

The highest, most jagged, and also most sacred peaks in Korea are in the Diamond Mountains, now located in North Korea, so I couldn't visit them. But in her Korean adventures, Isabella Bishop was determined to spend time in these fabled mountains. Since her party could not navigate sufficiently close by water to appreciate their stark beauty, she decided to go into the Diamond Mountains by horseback. It was a grueling but esthetically awesome journey.

After unpleasant experiences with officials and "literary swells" at Yong-chhun, the retinue returned down river. They had navigated the south fork of the Han as far as possible and were only able to catch glimpses of Soraksan. They then retraced the river to the town of Ma-chai, from which they took the north fork of the Han as far as it was navigable. It took some persuasion and cash, but the crew finally agreed to take the north branch of the river with its more frequent rapids, toward the Diamond Mountains. Her itinerary for this part of the journey is delineated in one of the two maps included as fold outs in *Korea and Her Neighbors*. It was a difficult journey. Just south of Nang-chon, where the north fork became no longer navigable, they left the sampan after five and a half weeks of challenge and ordeal on the branches of the Han River. From there they went overland by horseback into the Diamond Mountains.

They headed inland from the town of Paik-Kui Mi, where Isabella Bishop observed a wedding ceremony. This occasioned a digression on the institution of marriage in Korea, which was arranged, and in which a man confirmed his manhood and a woman continued her isolation and servitude under a different master. Isabella Bishop found several occasions in her book to comment on the difficulties of being a woman in Korea. She noted that conjugal fidelity was required of Korean women but not of men. (She made no mention of European customs on this score.) She also commented here, as elsewhere, on the isolation of upper-class Korean women from all society outside the home. After marriage, the bride was confined to the compound of her husband's family, and she lost her childhood identity.

> "The name bestowed on her by her parents soon after her birth is dropped, and she is known thereafter only as "the wife of so and so," or "the mother of so and so." Her husband addresses her by the word yabu, signifying "Look here," which is significant of her relations to him."[23]

For the trip into the Diamond Mountains, her party used miniature horses. She caricatured these Korean ponies as unruly and pugnacious. This part of her journey was clearly more uncomfortable than the previous river trip by sampan, despite the rapids and obstreperous villagers she had endured previously. Along with the ponies came several horse tenders, called *mapus,* who cared for the horses, urged them along when necessary, and tried, often unsuccessfully, to keep them from fighting.

> "My first experience of the redoubtable Korean pony was not reassuring. The men had never seen a foreign saddle and were half an hour in gett ing it "fixed." Though a pony's saddle, it was far too large for the creature's body. . . The animal bit, squealed, struck with his fore and hind feet, and performed the singular feat of bending his back into such an inward curve that his small body came quite near the

> ground. The men were afraid of him, and it was only in the brief intervals of fighting that they dared to make a dash at the buckles. . .
>
> They are most desperate fighters, squealing and trumpeting on all occasions, attacking every pony they meet on the road, never becoming reconciled to each other even on a long journey, and in their fury ignoring their loads, which are often smashed to pieces. Their savagery makes it necessary to have a mapu for every pony, instead of, as in Persia, one to five."[24]

Very few true roads existed; most were simply pony trails, often muddy or dusty and hard to follow. Moreover, since she didn't have a sampan for private sleeping quarters, Isabella was forced to avail herself of local inns, which she described with considerable repugnance.

> "On arriving at an inn, the master or servant rushes at the mud, or sometimes matted, floor with a whisk, raising a great dust, which he sweeps into a corner. The disgusted traveler soon perceives that the heap is animate as well as inanimate, and the groans, sighs, scratchings, and restlessness from the public room show the extent of the insect pest."[25]

Once her company came within view of the Diamond Mountains though, she waxed poetic at the sight of them.

> "[T]hrough the parting branches. . .were glimpses of granite walls and peaks reddening into glory; red stems, glowing in the slant sunbeams, lighted by the blue gloom of the conifers; there were glints of foam from the loud-tongued torrent below; the dew fell heavily, laden with aromatic

odors of pines, and. . .the picture was as fair as one could hope to see."[26]

The Diamond Mountains served as an important retreat for Buddhist monks in Korea, many of whom had fled into mountains throughout the peninsula after bouts of persecution by rulers of Koguryu and especially Yi dynasties. With few towns and no sampan, Isabella Bishop spent time in monasteries, which she vastly preferred over the local town inns.

Isabella Bishop experienced great peace and beauty in the Korean backcountry, especially in the mountains. As did I.

Soraksan National Park

Chapter 6

TEMPLES, TOMBS, AND TIME

In the late 1800s, the Diamond Mountains were strewn with Buddhist monasteries. Inhabiting these secluded and peaceful complexes were many men who wished to escape the cares of the world. They came to this idyllic region to lead a life uncomplicated by the stresses of city and family. Buddhist temples and monasteries had been banned from cities during the early Yi Dynasty, forcing followers of Gautama (The Buddha) into the mountainous countryside where many of their temples and shrines still stand.

Isabella Bishop stayed in monasteries during her foray into the Diamond Mountains. She found the monasteries infinitely more pleasant, not to mention cleaner, than the inns she had endured in other parts of the country. They were, however, over-heated—as were (and still are) most Korean dwellings. A monastery she considered particularly impressive was Chang-an Sa (*sa* means 'temple'). The restoration of this monastery apparently dated to the sixth century A.D., during the Silla Kingdom, Korea's longest dynasty.

> *"It is an exercise in forbearance to abstain from writing much about the beauties of Chang-an Sa as seen in two days of perfect heavenliness. It is a calm retreat, that small, green, semicircular plateau which the receding hills have left, walling in the back and sides with rocky precipices half*

> *clothed with forest, while the bridgeless torrent in front, raging and thundering among huge boulders of pink granite, secludes it from all but the adventurous. Alike in the rose of sunrise, in the red and gold of sunset, or gleaming steely blue in the prosaic glare of midday, the great rock peak on the left bank, one of the highest in the range, compels ceaseless admiration."*[27]

She remarked on the mixed iconography in temple wall paintings: interwoven images of Buddhist, Hindu and shamanistic symbolism. Here, too, being the only Western woman ever seen by the monks, pilgrims, and monastery workers, she was the subject of intense curiosity. She viewed Buddhists—outlawed in cities and scorned in most of the countryside—much more favorably than she did the "so-called followers of Confucius," such as yangban officials she had encountered during her travels.

The day after my tour of the peaks of Soraksan, I had planned to visit a Buddhist temple by foot and take a cable car to a fortress on a nearby peak. My plans were foiled by heavy rain, so I decided to save that experience for another visit, which never materialized. I returned to Camp Long in mid-afternoon, bought gas on the base, and held class that evening. The next morning I again left Wonju by car, this time to see ancient remains of the Silla Kingdom in the south.

Driving toward Kyongju, former capital of the Silla Kingdom, I was once again enchanted by the seemingly unspoiled beauty of mountains rising on the left as I drove south. Their beauty has only recently returned following the deforestation and military devastation of the first half of the twentieth century. The G.I.s who remember Korea from the war years and soon afterwards say that the mountains were mostly denuded of trees. These had been cut down for fuel in cold Korean winters and for timber to rebuild homes destroyed during the war and the prior Japanese occupation.

Much less ravaged was the area around Kyongju, which was protected during the Korean War by the Pusan Perimeter, a line held by the Allies throughout the conflict at great sacrifice to both U.N. troops and Koreans. Thus, Kyongju was preserved for posterity, in part through the stubbornness of General MacArthur who was determined to hold that line against any communist advance, regardless of cost.

Kyongju is probably the most historic city in all Korea, although it is now little more than a country town. From this place, the Silla monarchy ruled a large part of the southern Korean peninsula for nearly a thousand years. Initially, Silla was one of three major kingdoms dominating the peninsula--the others were Paekche and Koguryu. The latter is the term from which, in modified form, we derive the word Korea.

Isabella Bishop did not visit this region during her stay in the country. It was neither a trading city nor easily accessible by river. Perhaps it is just as well for the sake of Korean cultural preservation that Kyongju has been relatively inaccessible to travelers and conquerors alike. Despite the devastation wrought during four major military sweeps of the peninsula in the Korean War, Kyongju was spared, and a vast number of ancient structures and artifacts still exist in that city, which is now a living museum.

Huge, ancient, manicured grave mounds rise throughout the city and its surroundings, mimicking the gently sloping mountains that serve as backdrop. Temples, statues of Buddha, pagodas, and ruins of pleasure gardens are scattered among hills and rice paddies ringing the city. Also in Kyongju is an astronomical observatory built during the reign of Queen Sondok in the seventh century C.E. Koreans claim this as the oldest astronomical observatory in East Asia.

The Silla Kingdom lasted from the first century B.C.E. through most of the seventh century C.E., one of the longest continuous dynasties in world history. Until the advent of twentieth century aerial destruction, Korea had been relatively spared conquest by a combination of its peninsular geography and the logistical difficulties of waging warfare in mountainous terrain.

In the two millennia during which they have bulged from the terrain around Kyongju, nearly all tomb mounds from the Silla Kingdom have remained intact, testimony to the genuine reverence Koreans have for their ancestors. One of the mounds was recently opened by the tourist department of the city and made available for viewing; the tomb contents now reside in the municipal museum. Many grave mounds are clustered in Mounds Park, a combination of woods and lawns with mounds jutting like breasts from the ground, either singly or in double-humped pairs, the latter being graves of royal couples.

Mounds and Mountains, Kyongju

As I viewed the mounds against the mountainous backdrop, it was obvious that the mound builders had created little mountains that echoed the greater mountains in the distance where gods and spirits were thought to dwell. And I realized that the small grave hemispheres dotting mountainsides throughout the country were miniatures of these larger mounds, designed to retain spirits laid there to rest.

The National Kyongju Museum holds an extensive collection of Korean cultural artifacts dating back to the Neolithic Period. When I was there, very few labels or explanations were in English or in any other European language. I have been assured that this is no longer the case. I bought two English-language books on Kyongju; both were awkward translations of Korean tourist brochures and difficult to read although beautifully illustrated. Many other sites and historical monuments, including the opened tomb mound, can be visited in a two or three day sojourn. I again visited Kyongju while living in Taegu the following year and would like to have gone more often.

Within easy driving distance outside Kyongju is a magnificent Buddhist temple, Pulguksa, considered by many Koreans the most beautifully constructed and revered temple in the country. All the stonework is original, from the eighth century, but most of the wooden structures were destroyed during a Japanese invasion around 1600. The buildings were recently reconstructed, based upon ancient models and diagrams, and it is now a working temple as well as a popular destination for Korean tourists and Buddhist pilgrims.

A few miles from Pulguksa is Sokkuram, a grotto near the East Sea where a huge, ancient stone statue of Buddha sits facing east. This statue and the surrounding temple complex and access route were also constructed during the Silla period. The statue is said originally to have had a large diamond in its forehead (a third eye), which caught rays of the sun rising out of the sea, reflecting a holy and spectacular light upon everything around it. The diamond has long since disappeared—stolen, perhaps, because Koreans revere Buddha less than they revere their ancestors. It has been replaced by glass. Moreover, the great stone Buddha now sits behind a thick plastic shield for fear of vandalism. This hut separates his third (glass) eye from the rising sun. Thus we are left to imagine what magic might have astonished early pilgrims to the grotto.

Still, a general peace pervades the area in intervals between the throngs of clamoring school children. I was fortunate to watch a service held in the enclosed area. A Buddhist monk allowed a group of women entry into the plastic hut, and he held a ceremony with chanting and chiming. I experienced a sense of reverence while observing the ceremony and the space, even though I understood neither the words nor their symbolism.

A distracting feature of my trip to Kyongju and environs was the pervasive presence of school children. I tended to go slowly and let them pass when I wanted to savor a place. I was clearly viewed as strange by the children. One small child wrenched herself away from her mother in the Kyongju Museum and ran over to me. She then stood and stared at me in stupefaction. I encountered very few other Westerners (I remember only one) during both visits to Kyongju and vicinity.

In my two years of touring cultural sites throughout the country, it seemed that the majority of visitors were Korean school children on field trips. Buses would park in rows along the sides of the parking lot, dribbling or absorbing lines of youngsters. In most cases, the children of a group all wore a particular colored uniform—yellow or green or plaid—probably making them easier to keep track of by monitors. The children's ages ranged from preschoolers to older teens.

They were usually excited to see a Westerner. The girls might giggle, and a boy, perhaps the bravest, would come up, look at me, hold up a hand and say "Hello" or "Hi." If I smiled and responded, more children would approach, and I might soon be mobbed by school children trying out their spotty English and then dispersing after a few exchanges, tittering among themselves.

Once, as I was walking the grounds of a Buddhist temple, a boy of perhaps eleven or twelve, dressed in what appeared to be a Boy Scout uniform, began walking beside me. He was with a group of boys of comparable age who were not wearing uniforms. He didn't say much, but he smiled and seemed friendly, almost protective. Some of his companions dropped back from their swarm ahead of me and asked questions such as, "What's your name," or "Where do you live?" Eventually, one of the bolder ones asked, "How old are you," a question he had no doubt learned in English class.

In response to the question, I told the boys "sixty four" in English, which is how old I would have been in oriental tallying, although in Western reckoning I was sixty three. Koreans and most other Asians, including Chinese, count age differently than we do in the West. A child is one year old (in its first year) until the first birthday, at which time the child becomes two years old (in its second year). My companion did not understand sixty four in English, and I couldn't remember exactly how to say it in Korean. So I did a hand sign: first six fingers, and then four fingers. The boy in the scout uniform looked at me in surprise, and his eyes grew wide. He bowed deeply, then ran off to the group in front and said something in Korean that I recognized as sixty four. They chattered among themselves and moved on.

I imagine they all knew a few women in their sixties, no doubt bent and wobbly, who were surrounded and protected by doting family. Most Korean women my age were children during the Japanese occupation and are now small and rachitic, bow-legged from inadequate childhood nutrition, especially calcium, and permanently bent from long years of carrying children on their backs, cleaning the floors of their houses with short brooms, working in the fields, and serving their families. Finally, at age sixty, they are given a party by the family, at which time they are surrounded by food and gifts. After that, they have respected elder status and aren't expected to work much, except to care for their husbands.

One of the frequently asked questions that a Westerner can expect in Korea is, "How old are you?" In the West, this would be considered a rude question, especially if asked of a woman. But in Korea, as in other Confucian cultures, it's important to know a person's age in order to accord that person an appropriate level of respect. Small differences in age, particularly among children, can mean important differences in respect level. In fact, any time I had an exchange with a Korean that tended in the direction of friendship, an early question always was, "How old are you?"

When I told children how old I was, they would usually bow in a gesture of great respect and deference. Besides age, learning is highly respected, and learned persons are usually teachers. Adults often bowed when I told them I was a teacher. The Korean term *son sang nim* means both 'most honored person' and 'teacher.' Many Koreans I encountered considered biology a particularly difficult subject. I don't believe I ever met one who admitted to liking or doing well in biology. This could reflect something in the Korean mindset or in the way biology is taught in Korea. Or it might simply have been a self-effacing statement reflecting humility on the part of the speaker.

Hence, my Korean experiences and impressions continually reminded me that I was a woman of a certain age, and that I was a teacher, both of which were respected. This was in stark contrast to the pervading cultural ethos of my home country. The respect accorded to age and education made it possible for me to travel around the country by myself and to experience its many treasures and pleasures without fear.

Mobbed by school children in Kyongju

Chapter 7

CARS, BARS, AND MILITARY BASES

The culminating day of a week-long sequence of events, both mundane and bizarre, was strange indeed, even in the context of my often surreal life in Korea. It happened about a year after I had arrived in country and could be viewed as a metaphor for the jagged interface between the American military, their U.S. contractors, local Koreans, and persons of other nationalities imported to service the American military. Three background threads wove through the day as it unfolded: car problems, military regulations, and American night life in Korea.

It all began the afternoon the car wouldn't make it up hill 180 to the back gate of Osan AFB near my off-base apartment complex. The clutch had given me trouble for more than a month. So I wasn't exactly surprised when the car struggled but couldn't mount the hill, even in first gear.

It had been an excellent car for the price: dented, scarred and rusty on the outside, but the engine had always started and run smoothly, even in the bitter midwinter cold. The car had conveyed me and several colleagues back and forth to Camp Humphreys for two terms and to classes at Osan airbase almost daily. The car hauled boxes to the post office and laundry baskets to the laundromat, and it carried groceries and supplies back from the commissary and BX as needed.

Moreover, with an old car like the '88 Hyundai, I had no qualms about hauling preserved biology specimens and fluid lab supplies in the trunk, from the porches of my apartment to the high school lab and back every Friday evening for three terms. There was no permanent set-up on base for biology labs, so the instructor was required to store lab materials at home, transport them to an appropriate student facility for the lab, and then haul everything back afterwards. I felt a certain fondness for the car and would have gotten the clutch plate fixed, had I planned to stay in Osan.

But I was scheduled to leave Osan for Taegu, in the southern part of the peninsula, to teach at Camp Henry and other southern bases beginning in August. I had decided to buy another car, a newer and more reliable one—partly for moving to Taegu and partly for traveling around that region of the country. Several interesting cities—including Kyongju—lie in the southeastern part of the country. I had offered to buy a car from a UMUC colleague who wanted to sell it at the end of July. I was hoping mine would last until then. It didn't.

The process of deregistering (junking) a car on a military base is Byzantine. It is against regulations to own two cars with SOFA plates, and the old one must be sold or disposed of before buying the new one. I had bought and registered my car in Seoul at Camp Kim, the ROC camp associated with Yongsan. So I had to go back there (like Joseph to Bethlehem) in order to deregister the car, as directed by those in the know at the Osan Pass and ID office. I didn't normally have classes on Fridays, and I had planned to take a bus to Camp Kim either that Friday or the following one to turn in the license plates and paperwork. I then intended to buy the other car the following Monday.

I had recently gone to Yongsan, the major American military base in Seoul, to attend a panel discussion on the Korean War. I went early for that event so I could make a dry run for the car deregistration. (A logistical bent has stood me in good stead during this and many other adventures far from familiar ground.)

In Osan I had obtained information about the documents I would need to complete the process successfully. In Seoul, I went to Camp Kim to find the Pass and ID office for deregistering the car and to make sure I had all the information I needed. The wait there was about an hour, so I guessed that an hour was about the average Friday midday wait time, and I would need to factor that into my plans for the following week.

When the car wouldn't make it up the hill that Wednesday afternoon, I backed it down to a parking place in front of *Doksuri* (meaning 'eagle' in Korean), a set of upscale apartments on base where visiting generals and other dignitaries were quartered. I knew that gravity would help with the drive down the hill to the repair shop where official documents could be obtained for junking a car. Since no other cars were parked in front of Doksuri, I was mildly concerned about leaving the car, fearing it might be towed; there was no mistaking it for a general's car. A basket of clean laundry in the back seat also signaled a low-rank owner. Jim Williams, another faculty member with whom I normally carpooled to Camp Humphreys on Mondays and Wednesdays, picked me up on the hill and drove me to class that evening.

On Thursday I drove down the hill, obtained the documents I needed for Pass and ID, and had them notarized at the legal office. I then took them to the hobby shop, the on-base auto mechanic training, repair and play center. After a little more running around to get extra copies of a document, I got a stamp saying that the repair shop had the car and would dispose of it upon payment of the $75.00 disposal fee. They did give me the license plates, needed for the final process of deregistration in Seoul. At that point, the car was property of the U.S. government and would probably be passed on to some local junk dealer. But this turned out to be only half the hassle with the car.

Korea, Are You at Peace?

Another thread of the story involved a power outage at Camp Humphreys just before class on Wednesday. The power came back on half an hour later, but not before most students had left the classroom after voting to make up the class, including a test, on Friday. Since I no longer had a car, I didn't have a way to get to and from class on Friday, which was not a normal class day. When I mentioned my dilemma in the faculty lounge, Jim said that he and Steve Anderson were also going to Camp Humphreys on Friday for a make-up class, but they would be leaving the education building precisely at 7:30 pm, and I could ride back to Osan with them if I wanted to. Although this was more than an hour before normal class dismissal time, it was my best option since the last base bus between Humphreys and Osan left at 7:00 pm.

So on Friday, I went from Osan airbase to Yongsan Army Base in Seoul and from there to Camp Kim to officially deregister the old car. I then needed to return from Yongsan to Camp Humphreys, south of Osan, to teach the make-up class. I had also promised to arrive early at Humphreys for a help session for some students. It required a fairly tight sequence of bus connections and office hopping to do all that. In the plan, I had a buffer of about an hour for delays and unforeseen complications. And hopefully, lunch. True to the vicissitudes of military logistics, the bus schedule between bases had been changed, and the Pass and ID office at Camp Kim was short staffed. It was a photo finish, with me running to catch the last possible bus from Yongsan to Camp Humphreys. No lunch.

Once at Camp Humphreys, I bought a grape drink and Fritos to sustain me through the help session and test. Students received an assignment in lieu of the lecture I would normally have given after a test. I was outside the building by 7:20 pm in order to be on time for Jim's scheduled departure.

Steve and Bill Tillman were standing there waiting for Jim to come out. Steve gingerly broached the subject of what the guys *really* planned to do after class. They wanted to go bar hopping in Anjunri, a district near Camp Humphreys dotted with places that catered to the military. Apparently that part of town had a reputation for action, and the guys intended to have a few beers and check it out. I wasn't crazy about the idea of bar hopping but went along since I was definitely in the minority. Not wanting to be a spoilsport, and having no other ride home, I simply said, "Sure, I'll go along. It might be an adventure." As it turned out, I had a chance to see a side of single male life in Korea I would not otherwise have experienced.

I had heard stories about the Songtan bar life from John, with whom I shared the Hyundai while he was teaching at Osan; he liked to bar-hop and he liked to talk. From him and from a female colleague back in the U.S., I had heard about the "juicy girls" who worked in the bars—mostly young women from the Korean countryside or from other countries such as the Philippines. The owners and operators of bars around military bases go out into the countryside, and even to other countries, to recruit girls to work in their establishments. They give the girls—often their families—money up front for them to come to town and work in the bars. The girls then owe that money to the establishment and are required to work it off. This is, in fact, a form of indentured servitude with overtones of white slavery. The girls work by sitting with patrons in the bars—mostly G.I.s and other male expatriates—and asking the men to buy them drinks, usually just fruit juice, at exorbitant prices.

In the meantime, the girls rack up more debt for food, clothes and lodging, so they become tied to the establishment unless they can find some G.I. who will buy them out. According to John, they were also able to earn extra money by sleeping with patrons, although that was presumably not official policy. Whether the establishment received any revenue from that income wasn't clear.

The first bar we went into in Anjunri was pretty tame. It had only two small rooms, a front room with tables and chairs and a back room with pool tables. We sat in the front room; the guys all ordered beers and I ordered *saida*—a carbonated Korean soda. We were the only patrons in the room. The guys didn't go into the back room, although one woman with a pool cue poked her head around the door. My presence may have inhibited the women from coming on to the guys.

The second bar we visited had a large central room with two pool tables and a stage. A bikini-clad woman in high heels danced a writhing, sensuous routine on stage. Rimming the central room was an elevated platform with tables and chairs where a few people were sitting and having drinks. We ordered the same drinks as before. Black lights around the walls cast an eerie glow, transforming white clothing to purple as people sat or moved about. The central stage was well lit, and the dancers, who changed every five or ten minutes, were mostly Caucasians. Jim and Bill said they were probably Russians. Steve seemed surprised to hear that. Bill explained that it's common for Russian women to work as dancers in Korean bars. He claimed that Korean men will pay many *won* (₩) for a Caucasian woman. Vladivostok is nearby and this was a way Russians could earn enough money to live on, as the Russian economy had tanked with the collapse of the USSR.

There was a sign outside indicating "Servicemen Only," so it was not surprising that most patrons in this bar were G.I.s. A few Koreans, perhaps ROK soldiers, were drinking at side tables. A Korean woman was snuggling up to the crotch of an American, who was not in uniform, on a bench not far from the door. After we sat down, Jim went to find a snack so he wouldn't become too drunk to drive. As he came back to the table, he heard the hostess ask the American to either pay or leave, saying the girl had been "lap dancing" with him for a long time. The hostess was a middle-aged Korean woman (*ajuma*, meaning 'auntie'), apparently typical in such establishments, and she handled things firmly. The American walked out.

The third bar we went into, called Bay Watch, was a very large room with the stage at the end farthest from the door. Again, attractive women in bikinis or G-strings danced on stage, this time around a pole. Next to us was a table full of very friendly Russian women, one of whom took a picture of the four of us with my camera. The hostess, again a Korean ajuma, wore a traditional Korean outfit, so this was evidently a classier place than the others. At one point, a G.I. came in wearing a hat with strips of toilet paper tucked into the hat band and fluttering over the brim. This outraged Steve ("damned disrespectful Americans"), who almost got up and started a fight with him. Jim calmed him down by suggesting that perhaps it was a protest against the lack of toilet paper in most Korean toilets; the man was visibly bringing his own.

According to Bill, the places we went were pretty tame compared with Itaewon, the district of Seoul near Yongsan Army Base. Bill had lived in Seoul, and though he was married and had a family back in the States, he frequented the bar scene and appreciated oriental women—as do many American males. In Korea, as well as in Southeast Asia and Japan, women are very deferential toward men. As Steve remarked, "I have a friend in Taegu who wants to see to it that my life is as easy and pleasant as possible." He also quoted an American friend as saying, "I'll never marry another Caucasian woman."

None of my colleagues made passes at any of the women in the bars, and we came back to our apartment complex in Songtan at a reasonable hour. I was probably the wet blanket on any fire that might have ignited between the guys and the bar girls, but the men seemed content just to drink and watch.

By contrast, John, the colleague with whom I had owned the now defunct car, had become actively involved with two bar girls in Songtan, and even became so obsessed with one that he went to her village when she didn't show up in the bar for about a week. I knew all of this because he talked endlessly of his exploits. He seemed to view me as an older sister to whom he could confess his feelings and brag about his activities.

The Western male in the East has the best of all possible worlds. He has the expatriate's freedom from serious responsibility and the easy availability of sweet, compliant Asian women, to which Rudyard Kipling alluded in his poem *Mandalay*.

> . . .neater, sweeter maiden in a cleaner, greener land!. . .
> With 'er arm upon my shoulder an' 'er cheek against my cheek. . .
> If you've 'eard the East a-callin' you won't never 'eed naught else.

It becomes an addictive lifestyle for many western males. I saw them in airports, in restaurants, and on the street—wherever I traveled in Asia. These men were in their 30s to 60s, usually with a beer belly and unkempt appearance, swaggering and confident, a lovely young oriental woman often on their arm or across the table at a restaurant. I confess they were an embarrassment to me.

While probably not so degenerate, many of the military males were almost as predatory as non-military expatriates. They assumed that the sexy, available Eastern females were there for their use and amusement. Some military men do ultimately marry Korean girlfriends, especially if they become pregnant. It may be one of the goals of the girls, at least those living near military bases, to catch an American husband and escape the impoverished and confined life they would otherwise lead as females in Korea.

The seamier side of British and Korean cultural interaction was apparently not witnessed by Isabella Bishop. Or if it was, she didn't report on it. Of course her main contacts were missionaries, not soldiers or military contractors.

Chapter 8

MONSOON

When my car stalled in the middle of a throughway exit during a monsoon torrent in late July, my skimpy Korean language skills, painfully accumulated until then, were useless.

Korea lies in that part of Asia termed by geographers "monsoon Asia." This area includes the rim of lowlands in southern and eastern Asia that lie between the surrounding oceans (Indian and Pacific) and the high Mongolian plateau of central Asia. That high, dry plateau becomes hot in the summer, and its rising air draws winds from the oceans bordering the lowlands, carrying with it moisture that can condense into torrential rains in summer. The countries of monsoon Asia are lush, not arid like those on the western and northern sides of the plateau. And they are able to sustain abundant vegetation despite millennia of human habitation and farming.

Indeed, the monsoons can be both a blessing and a curse, increasing agricultural productivity, while sometimes washing away villages and cropland along river valleys. Monsoon rains in July of 1995 caused flooding and devastation throughout North Korea, resulting in a near collapse of that already fragile economy not long after Kim Jong-il came to power. As a consequence, North Korea was forced to call for help from the international community. Humanitarian aid groups were temporarily allowed into the country and soon discovered the extent of deprivation suffered by the population even before the natural disaster. Serious floods occurred again recently, in August, 2012, not long after Kim Jong-un came to power. This Kim has resorted to threats rather than appeals for aid. Perhaps he believes the DPRK military might and nuclear weapons can coerce resources for his country by threat of force.

Isabella Bishop experienced the fury of the rains in this region of monsoon Asia during her second year there. After coming out of the Diamond Mountains, she took a Japanese steamer from Wonsan to Pusan. There she encountered rumors of rebellion and impending war, signaled by an increased Japanese show-of-force in the port. She then traveled to Inchon and found, to her dismay, an international military fleet (Japanese, American, French, Russian and Chinese) lying at anchor in the harbor. Troops crowded the Japanese quarter.

Fearing an immediate outbreak of war, the British vice-consul asked her to leave Korea immediately. She was forced to flee, departing without traveling gear (most of which had been left at Wonsan) and without "civilized luggage," passport, or money (left in Seoul). She obtained some money and clothing through the combined kindnesses of the British consul and the wife of the Spanish minister at Chefoo (Chi Fu) after she arrived in China.

From China, she traveled to Manchuria, much of which was Russian territory at that time. She took the Hun-ho River on her way to Mukden from Neuchwang, and it was during this river trip that she experienced the extremity of monsoon rains.

This was the first time she became really ill during her journey in Asia: fevers, headache, muscle and joint pain. The weather was severe; the boat was pelted with winds and rain for four days; and, although ill, she endured living and sleeping in soaked clothing and drinking *the "liquid cholera" of the flood.*[28]

There were record floods in the area at that time, and many

villages were washed away by high river water. She described her low point thus:

> "[T]he rain fell more tremendously than ever, and the strong wind, sweeping through the rigging with a desolate screech, only just overpowered the clatter on the roof. I was ill. The seas we shipped drowned the charcoal, and it was impossible to make tea or arrowroot. The rain dripped everywhere through the roof. My lamp spluttered and went out and could not be relighted, bedding and clothing were soaked, my bed stood in the water, the noise was deafening.
> Never in all my journeys have I felt so solitary."[29]

My own monsoon adventure happened about a year after I arrived in Korea, on a weekend after driving from Osan to Taegu with a colleague. I needed to move things—mostly lab supplies—into my new apartment there, and Steve had volunteered to help. He had spent two previous terms teaching in Taegu and liked the city. He said he had a friend there who could also help with unloading the car. Originally, I had assumed we would spend the night in Taegu on Saturday: me at my apartment and he with his friend. But when I asked him, he said he thought we would be coming back that night. I soon learned that Steve was not forthcoming about intentions and not a very reliable decision maker.

In June I had bought another car, a 1990 Daewoo Espero from a colleague I trusted. The car was in good condition and he said it should make road trips comfortably and without problems. He had replaced the battery and the alternator and had had a brake job done. When I took the car out for a test drive, the engine ran well, so I happily paid him $800 for it.

On the way down the peninsula to Taegu with Steve, the car handled beautifully. The ride was pleasant, the weather was sunny, and Steve was a regaling travel companion. We shared life stories, and about halfway through the trip, it came out that Steve was gay, despite two prior marriages and two daughters. He had met his friend Jong in a gay karaoke bar in Taegu, lived with him while teaching there, and saw him most weekends in Songtan, where Jong would arrive by bus from Taegu. I wondered out loud why Steve hadn't planned to spend the night with him in Taegu. He admitted that he *had* planned to stay but hadn't wanted to tell me about his friend.

In Taegu we discovered that Jong was very tired. He had stayed up until 6:00 am that morning, although he was willing to help with the moving. Ultimately, Steve made the decision to come back with me. It would have been better for both of us had we stayed that night in Taegu.

Jong was some help moving things into the apartment, but in other ways, he was a distraction. Steve acted like a kid around him, so it truly disrupted the rhythm of the job. I had no time to organize my apartment because Jong needed lunch. They moved some things into the apartment that I had intended to leave in the car, complicating business I needed to negotiate that afternoon at the UMUC Education Center.

Steve and I left Taegu around 5:30 pm and had an easy drive until dusk. We made good time and were not far from Pyongt'aek when we saw lightning in the distance.

Steve remarked, "I miss a good summer storm from time to time."

I mused, "I thought we were supposed to have monsoon rains this time of year. I haven't seen anything so far that resembles a monsoon."

Then the sky opened up and delivered on both our wishes and our expectations. The hard rain started right after we passed Chosin. The traffic slowed to 20 kph in the pelting rain. I had the windshield wipers on maximum speed but could catch only brief glimpses of the road ahead. My strategy was to stay in my lane and follow the taillights of the car ahead at a distance of several car lengths. This worked well. The traffic kept moving, albeit slowly. In one of the flashes of clear vision, I saw an exit sign for Pyongt'aek and said to Steve, "We're almost there. Our exit is next."

He mused, "We should be back by 9 o'clock."

At that point, traffic slowed even more. We saw an overhead sign for "Osan, 6 km." Shortly thereafter, traffic came to a complete halt for about five minutes and then began inching forward at a snail's pace. The rain actually let up a bit, so we could see lines demarcating the lanes. People began jockeying for whichever lane seemed to be going slightly faster. Steve tried to persuade me to get into one of the left lanes, which were moving somewhat more quickly, but I wanted to stay in the right lane because I knew we would need to exit soon, and I didn't want to be trapped on the left. As it happened, the whole issue was moot.

All traffic soon came to a complete stop. We kept the engine running for about twenty minutes, thinking we would probably move soon. The air conditioner was working, which made the damp and stuffy car interior tolerable. But we didn't move. Then the water started to rise. When I opened the car door I saw water rushing two inches below its edge. The water was dense and muddy; leaves and fragments of plastic bobbed on its surface. I was afraid to turn off the engine for fear it wouldn't start again. On the other hand, the gas gauge was inching lower as the engine kept running. I finally turned off the engine. Although we had enough gas to get back to Osan, I didn't want to run the tank down to empty. I always carried a five gallon spare can of gas in the trunk, but I didn't want to pour it into the gas tank in the drenching rain standing calf deep in water.

So we sat there in the dark, in the rain, with the waters rushing around us, boxed in on all sides. The cars of impatient drivers clogged the shoulder so that even emergency vehicles could not get through. A tow truck with a car in tow tried to use the right shoulder, but it couldn't move either. The banter and humor that had enlivened most of the trip were reduced to occasional, strained comments: sometimes of hope, sometimes of resignation. Of course I was wishing we had spent the night in Taegu.

Finally, after more than an hour of immobility, the far left lane began to inch forward. Every car in the whole clogged mass lurched and veered to get into that lane. I cranked the starter and, to my relief, the engine chugged to life. We also tried to edge over to the left despite our upcoming exit on the right. Slowly, slowly, the cars began to move; no one around us ran into anyone else; and only one nearby car was stalled. We eventually made it into the left lane and were able to move ahead from there. Soon, policemen with light sticks directing traffic became visible through the shroud of rain.

As we hit the bottleneck, I realized what had happened. A mudslide from a hill on the right formed a barrier three or four feet tall and several yards wide, completely closing off traffic going in our direction. I wondered how many cars had gotten caught under the mud itself. Earth movers had cleared one lane (a back-hoe tractor was visible up the road beyond the barrier), and that single lane allowed a trickle of traffic to pass through.

However, the mud barrier had created a dam, and water accumulated behind it. That water rushed through the narrow opening and spread out downhill like rapids, carrying mud and debris with it. As we passed through the bottleneck, the deeper water behind the dam rushed along the sides of the car and splashed up over the hood. I knew enough from experiences with Charleston floods to keep the gas pedal down and the engine running no matter what.

The car made it through the deepest part of the torrent, but on the other side, it began choking and sputtering. Then it seemed to run more smoothly as we sped up, but I could barely see light from the headlamps. A sign overhead read "Osan, 2 km."

Steve said, "Well, at least we'll be home by midnight."

Fatal pronouncement. As I slowed down to pay at the toll booth, the car again started to choke and sputter, and I had to put it into neutral and rev the engine to keep it going. Beyond the toll booth, cars were backed up in the two left turn lanes for Osan and Songtan. The engine was still behaving strangely and the gas gauge had crept down to empty. I was afraid the car was so low on gas that water at the bottom of the tank was causing the engine to run rough. I decided to refill the gas tank while we were waiting for traffic lanes to move.

Steve asked, "Are you going to put in gas while the car is running?"

I said, "Yes, I'm afraid if we let it die it won't start again."

I asked him to move over into the driver's seat and keep his foot on the accelerator. I had another car key, which I could use to open the trunk and get the gas can. However by the time I had finished putting gas into the tank, Steve was out of the car offering to help. I was really annoyed and told him that the way to help was to keep the car running. Then I realized it was not. And there was no starting it again.

After putting up the hood and setting a reflecting triangle behind the car, we went to a gas station across the street. I carried with me a Korean dictionary and a road-help phrase sheet, both of which I always kept in the glove compartment. When I tried to say something about the "car not going," the attendant stared at me blankly, so I pointed to a phrase in the booklet to the effect "I am in trouble; my car won't work." He just smiled. This was when I realized the utter inadequacy of my grasp of the Korean language.

Steve then drew a picture of a tow truck and car on the white board in the office. The man looked at that, called his boss, they chatted a bit, and they both shrugged. Steve used his cell phone to call Jong in Taegu, hoping that *he* might be able to explain our predicament to the gas-station attendant. After much back and forth between Steve and Jong and the attendant, the upshot was that there were no tow trucks available, and we were stuck.

I decided to try another station in view down the road. As I walked toward it, Steve lagging behind, I saw a car stopped nearby. I looked into the window and realized that the car's occupants were Westerners—probably American military. I walked toward them with what they later told me was a very worried look on my face.

The driver rolled down his window and asked, "Are you having some trouble?"

I said, "Yes, indeed. Do you happen to be from Osan airbase?"

He said, "No, we're from Yongsan. But we're going to Osan. Do you need a ride?"

It happened that only one of them, the driver, was American military. The other two were his brother and his son; they were going to Osan to use the gym there for a late night work-out! The driver said, "If you need a ride, I guess we could squeeze you in."

By this time, Steve had arrived. He explained that we had a car sitting in the middle of the street that we needed to do something about. So he and the three guys went back to the car, while I went to the other gas station to try the phrase-book routine, again without success.

After this further ineffectual attempt at communication with a gas station attendant, the guys decided they would push the car out of the road. I got behind the wheel while Steve stopped traffic, taking his life in his hands in the middle of a monsoon, and the three other guys pushed. The car moved quickly, and I steered it into a vacant lot next to the gas station. The passenger side windows were both open and wouldn't close because they were electrically operated, but by that time the rain had slowed. I decided not even to worry about it.

We all crowded into the other car and started—very slowly—in the direction of Osan. As we made the left turn toward the airbase, we saw a couple, soaking wet, holding hands and walking in the same direction we were driving. They looked like Americans; probably they had had car trouble too. Every once in a while we would catch up with them, but then they would walk on ahead again, an indication of how slowly traffic was moving. Steve was ready to wager they would beat us to Songtan, about five miles away. But our driver pulled some fascinating maneuvers, including driving down one of the oncoming lanes for two or three blocks, declaring it a "SOFA lane."

At one badly blocked intersection, he pulled all the way into the far left lane for oncoming traffic and around a truck, only to find a Korean policeman directing traffic at the intersection. He pulled out in front of the stopped truck then zigzagged into the far right lane as the policeman furiously waved his nightstick at us. Then he zipped behind a truck coming in from the cross street and ahead into the traffic going toward Songtan and out of view of the policeman. "Let him come after me," was all he said.

It soon became clear why traffic was moving so slowly in the direction we were heading. After the cut-off to the old section of Osan, the road passed through low-lying rice fields, and several sections were flooded. Perhaps the water was not as deep as at the landslide bottleneck, but in places it was the depth we had been stalled in just south of the exit. On the roadsides everything was flooded. The river had overflowed its banks and acres of rice plants were completely submerged. I was sure everything would be washed away or silted over—that nothing was likely to survive that flood. Three weeks later, I found out I was wrong; rice was growing nicely in those very same fields.

Even if we had managed to keep *my* car running, I doubt it would have made it through those submerged roadways. Fortunately, we were in a good car, driven by a knowledgeable, determined driver, and we made it back to Osan airbase, which was built on an elevated area.[30] Our American cowboy stopped at the Main Gate. We got out of the car, thanked him, and made the short walk back to our Jeung-eun apartment complex in Songtan. It felt as if we had been rescued by an angel of mercy.

The next day, I walked to the base auto repair shop and asked if they had a tow truck available to tow my car from Osan. The tow truck driver was having a day off, but he came in—perhaps out of pity for my flood story—and drove me to Osan, charged my car's battery for a while, and then followed me back to the shop, whereupon the car stalled again. So I left it there to be fixed. Eventually, they found a slight electrical leak around the battery and fixed it. Perhaps it just needed to dry out. I was able to retrieve it in two days and paid only forty dollars for the repairs.

Later, during a trip to Australia, I picked up some Australian money and brought it back for the tow-truck driver, which was all he said he wanted in return for the favor to me on his day off. Much of the trick of getting by in unfamiliar and difficult situations involves not losing heart, muddling through, and thankfully accepting the good luck of unexpected help from strangers.

Chapter 9

TAEGU, WHERE THE LIVIN' AIN'T EASY

It was easy to walk around or drive in Songtan without getting very lost. After some practice, I could recognize streets and landmarks near Osan airbase. Thus, if I became lost in town that first year, I was eventually able to figure out how to return to my apartment.

The second year in Korea, I lived in Taegu, a large city in the south of the peninsula, whose streets and byways were a maze I never felt able to navigate. I could find my way home from major highways connected to the Kyongbu Expressway—the main north-south route between Seoul and Pusan. But I was uneasy exploring much outside a swath of the city between Camp Walker (containing most base facilities), Camp Henry (where I taught most classes), and Camp George (where Biology labs were held at the high school). This area was about two miles long and a mile wide; I lived essentially in the middle of it and could walk to either Camp Walker or Camp Henry. I also had a car and could drive if necessary, especially to get groceries, to do laundry, or to transport lab supplies to Camp George.

The Korean language was still a constant challenge, as I was so frequently thrust into interactions with Koreans in that large and complex city. In the fall I audited an elementary Korean class taught through UMUC, and this helped some with vocabulary and grammar. Still, my understanding didn't go much beyond occasional words of an overheard conversation or the radio. I was ashamed to have been in the country so long without understanding more of its language.

Living in Taegu was much less pleasant than living in Songtan, so this colored my impressions of Korea during that last year. Taegu was a big city with big city problems: parking, noise, congestion, pollution. Having grown up in rural Michigan, I'm simply not fond of big cities. Moreover, large Korean cities proved particularly noisome. Even small Korean cities—or large towns such as Songtan—had little about them that was redeeming. They were a jumble of jerry-built shops and houses lining narrow, crooked alleyways crammed with cars and strewn with people meandering nonchalantly down the middle of the street because there were no sidewalks. Intersections were rarely perpendicular, so it was quite easy to become turned around going from one place to another. And there were almost no street names or signs. Even on maps, locations were generally indicated by names of hotels and businesses along the street or at intersections,

Street scene in Taegu

Korean drivers speed through traffic as if they were just short of insane when behind the wheel of a car. Adding to the hazards of the road are small, two-wheeled, motorized vehicles—neither motorcycles nor mopeds, but something in between—whose drivers know no rules whatsoever, but drive on roads and sidewalks indifferently, often going against traffic, weaving in and out of whatever bottleneck exists in front of them, a back wheel rack loaded with cargo, and a bag of goods often hanging from a hand stretched out to one side.

If driving was bad, parking was worse. In Taegu, as in all Korean cities I visited, there were too many cars and not enough parking spaces. People park anywhere—on the few sidewalks that exist, along traffic lanes of major highways because most have no shoulders, and along both sides of smaller two-way roads and alleyways, leaving room in the middle for only one car.

When cars meet going in opposite directions on these smaller roads, one car is required to pull over into a driveway or alleyway and allow the other to pass before driving on. Pedestrians and shopkeepers sometimes get into the act, helping drivers navigate narrow spaces. On the whole, I was able to maneuver through the tight squeezes left between parked cars, but I had a difficult encounter once with a Korean woman driver coming in the opposite direction. She wouldn't back up and I couldn't back up without risking my side view mirror already overhanging the window of the car parked to my right. Finally, a Korean bystander, trying to help the other woman, got into her car and backed it up so I could pass.

For parking, my initial strategy was to park where I saw other cars parked. That usually worked, but sometimes I would come back to my car and find an angry note decorating the windshield, or a woman might charge out from a shop and yell at me. Once I was called out of my apartment and asked to move my car by men who were doing work on the nearby alleyway. To avoid parking headaches, I often left the car on base at Camp Walker and walked back and forth when it wasn't raining or when I didn't need the car for errands. I eventually found a promising parking spot not far from the apartment along a major highway. It was always lined with parked cars and therefore seemed safe.

One day, after a month in Taegu, I had done some errands at Camp Walker in the afternoon. It was raining lightly, so I parked the car on the "safe" street and spent a couple hours in my apartment, intending to drive to class that evening. When I returned to pick up the car, it had disappeared. Another car, a white one, was in the spot where I thought I had left my black Daewoo. I walked up a block, thinking perhaps I had forgotten exactly where I parked it. No Daewoo Espero was to be seen anywhere along the street. To get to class on time, I took a taxi to Camp Henry. Inside the gate, some military police (MPs) drove by in a security vehicle, and I flagged them down to tell the story of my disappearing car. One suggested I go to the gate after class and call Security.

So after class I did just that. It turned out that Security was at Camp Walker. Security sent an MP in a car to pick me up at Camp Henry and take me back to Camp Walker. The desk sergeant there was very nice and said it happened all the time. I didn't know my license plate number, but I thought it had a couple of sixes and a seven in it because a workman had once come to my apartment complex and called out 'six' *(yuk)* and 'seven' *(chil)* in Sino-Korean when trying to find the owner (me) to move the car. The desk sergeant asked an MP to drive me to the apartment to get copies of the registration. By the time I returned to Security, and he looked at my paperwork, the Korean liaison officer had already found the car based on information I had given them. It had been towed to a lot in the middle of the city.

The person at the security desk asked a KATUSA (Korean Augmented Troops of the U.S. Army) soldier to drive me to the vehicle impoundment site to pick up my car. We got into his big black Hum-V topped with red-white-and-blue lights, which he left flashing during our entire ride. On the way, the Korean soldier asked me to show him where I had parked the car. I directed him to where my car had been, and we parked nearby. The white car was still there. He pointed to a Korean street sign behind the white car and translated. "No parking for 300 meters."

I told him that the white car had been there when I was looking for mine five hours earlier. We walked over to the car, and he pointed to a sign in Korean inside the windshield. This read, "Sorry, I will be right back."

I asked him what the rules actually were. He answered, "The rules are what the policeman thinks."

We went to the vehicle impoundment site and bailed out my car, which cost ₩80,000 (about $80). They didn't give me a ticket, just a slip of paper with the cost on it. I found out later that it's so complicated to write out tickets for cars with SOFA license plates that they simply tow them without giving a ticket. The next day, I asked a Korean office worker to make a sign in Korean saying: 'Sorry, I'll be right back.' After that, I usually parked the car at Camp Walker or Camp Henry and used my sign when parking on the street.

For a few days after the towing episode, I was seething with anger. As I walked back and forth from home to one base or another, sometimes at night, often in the rain, my mind raged with contempt for Koreans and their attitude of rush-rush-then-sit-around-and-do-nothing (play golf or cards, talk with buddies, drink soju); for the slipshod, ill planned city of Taegu with its crowded, ugly streets; for the smell of rotting garbage and sewage wafting up from cracks in sidewalks and alleyways; for the (pen)insular mindset that just wants to be left to its own ways; for the karaoke culture; for the whining, sleazy looking women; for the arrogant, gravel-voiced, soju-drinking men.

Then one day, as I was walking to Camp Henry, a little boy ran out from a shop onto the sidewalk in front of me. He turned toward me and said, "Hello" and smiled.

I said, "Hello" and then *"Anyong hasseyo,"* the standard Korean greeting meaning 'Are you at peace?'

He smiled again and jumped up and down. He ran back into the shop and said something in an excited voice to the adult inside. The anger in me simply melted.

A few days later, I went into a local shop that sold good quality, wooden Korean furniture and trays. The shopkeeper, a woman, was very pleasant. Mrs. Kim eventually became my best friend in Taegu. We knew very little of each other's language, but we tried to communicate with good will. She helped me carry a couple pieces of furniture back to my apartment, and we exchanged phone numbers.

Later that evening, the lady upstairs brought me some Korean cake. I thought she said 'birthday' in Korean and pointed to the baby on her back. I later picked up a toy on base for the baby and took it to her, saying in my fractured Korean, "Baby birthday present." (*Agi sang-il son-mul*). The next day, she brought down some Korean food. Thus, I eventually developed a positive rapport with some Koreans in Taegu—although mostly with women and children who were willing to be kind.

A source of repeated irritation during the year in Taegu was the random, shoddy way things were constructed. When I first moved into the apartment, I noticed mildew on the back wall of one of the rooms and a long crack in another wall. Later when we had a heavy rain, the mildew spread, and the cracked wall developed a large black spot of mold. Obviously, the outside walls leaked, and water was seeping through.

Early in my stay there, the light in the bathroom began flickering. I thought perhaps I should change the light bulb but didn't get around to it. When I turned it on one day, the light began to spark. I looked up and saw smoke coming from above the partly dangling fixture. I immediately turned off the light and called the landlord's daughter, who spoke English reasonably well. I explained the situation.

This happened on a Thursday, the day before Chusok, the most important, week-long Korean holiday. The landlord was a baker whose specialty was Chusok cakes, so his daughter asked if I would wait until after the holidays for the repair. I replied, "I guess I'll have to."

I didn't dare turn on the light in the bathroom for fear of starting a fire, so I performed my ablutions for a week and a half in a dim light that penetrated the one square foot window high on the bathroom wall.

The landlord finally arrived with a screwdriver and electrician's tape and unscrewed the broken fixture, saying he'd come back the next day with a new fixture. His daughter had said he was going to get a good quality fixture, which sounded fine to me. This daughter did all of the translating between us until she and I became friendly. I think her father may have decided to put a stop to our communication; subsequent interactions with her father became increasingly difficult.

He came over the following day with the old fixture in hand, trying to remove a screw that had rusted into it. He wasn't able to do this, so he simply wired in a new socket he had brought—with no fixture—and screwed in a new bulb. He pointed at the lit bulb dangling from the ceiling by wires and looked at me hopefully. "OK?" All Koreans know "OK"

I said, "Not OK." I added what I hoped was the Korean equivalent, *"Anchohayo."*

I would have been afraid to take a shower with that bare bulb and its dangling wires hanging from the ceiling, incompletely covered with insulation. Korean bathrooms are, in fact, showers as well as toilets. Shower water from an overhead spigot sprays and drains down through a hole in the middle of the floor. I tried to make the point that taking a shower would be dangerous with the bare bulb hanging like that. He turned on the shower water and said "OK," getting my bathroom rug wet in the process. I removed his hand from the faucet, but not before the bathroom rug was drenched. I looked up at the bulb and shook my head. He looked at me sideways as if to say, *That's the best I'm going to do*. Then he left the apartment.

I stood in the bathroom and stared at the naked bulb. It looked so ugly. I thought nervously about taking a shower, water splashing onto the wiring. My landlord must have sensed my grief because he came back into the apartment and, seeing me still staring up at the bulb, he said, "Changee." Another word most Koreans know.

I said, "Yes, *Ye, Ne*" and he left again.

About half an hour later, he came back with a new fixture and installed it. That fixture immediately came down again because the ceiling was constructed of thickened, laminated pasteboard. Koreans don't seem to have the kind of expanding nut that will stay put in such thin partitions. Again, one of the wires was exposed. So, he rewrapped the wire with electrician's tape and reinstalled the fixture, with me standing on a chair next to him, both helping and monitoring. That fixture came down again later, but I fixed it myself with some screws and expanding bolts purchased on base, and it held for the duration of my stay.

Near the end of December that year, I returned to Charleston for the Christmas holidays. I explained to friends and family that Korea tends to have very little snow in winter, although it becomes quite cold. It has to do with winter monsoon winds that blow out of the Mongolian-Siberian high plateau. These winds contain little moisture but are very cold. This is in contrast to the water-laden summer monsoon winds, which flow from the Pacific Ocean toward the high central Asian plateau.

Winter winds also transport a fine, abrasive, dust-like sand from the high plateau that drifts into northern China and Korea. The loess thus deposited contributes greatly to the fertility of soil in these regions. My first winter there, I didn't understand why my car was so often covered with an amber film that had to be wiped from the windshield and left a brown smear from windshield wipers during a rain.

After declaring that Korea normally had very little winter snow, I came back to a winter of record snows. Temperatures were colder that winter than in any year since 1949, and Korea had more snow than in any year since 1964. Koreans were unaccustomed to that much snow, and the city of Taegu was inadequately equipped for it with salt, sand, or snow-plows. After a snow, the roads became a death trap. As far as I could judge, Koreans didn't modify their devil-take-the-hindmost driving style in inclement weather.

For me, this was a new experience, despite growing up in Michigan and living for six years in Syracuse, New York, where snows are sometimes several feet deep in winter. I'll admit, the Korean adventure began to wear very thin that winter, not so much because of the snow but because of heating problems.

Indeed, the heating system in my apartment in Taegu was not up to the challenge of a record cold spell, and the boiler stopped working. Three times. The first time was before I left for the U.S. on Christmas holiday. After threats that I wouldn't pay the rent if it didn't work, the landlord fixed the heater the day before I left. On my return, I had heat for a day or two, and then we had a record cold snap. The temperature fell below zero, Fahrenheit, which is about minus twenty degrees Celsius (-20° C). Everything froze. The boiler, which provided hot water for the sink faucets, the shower, and the floor heating system (*ondol* heating) was situated outside the apartment on a small, open, cement porch. Of course the boiler froze. In my apartment in Songtan, where experiences with apartment and landlord were infinitely more pleasant than in Taegu, the boiler was on an enclosed porch and had given no trouble during the previous winter.

Ondol heating is the preferred method of domestic heating in Korea. Steam or hot air circulates through pipes under the floor, rather than in wall ducts or radiators as in the West. This type of heating was used in all Korean homes, apartments, and yogwans I visited in Korea. It apparently derives from an earlier custom, still practiced in country villages, of passing the flue from the kitchen fire under the floor of other rooms of the house, thus serving as the major home heating.

This can become very hot in summer as Isabella Bishop mentioned repeatedly in her Korean travel memoir. She found it suffocating in summertime to sleep in a room that was still heated by effluent from the kitchen fire. She described overheated rooms in village inns during the first part of her journey along the Han River.

> "The room was always overheated from the...fire. From 80° to 90° was the usual temperature, but it was frequently over 92° and I spent one terrible night sitting at my door because it was 105° within. In this furnace, which heats the floor and the spine comfortably, the Korean wayfarer revels."[31]

When she stayed at Chang-an Sa, the much more pleasant Buddhist monastery in the Diamond Mountains, she again described sleeping on uncomfortably overheated floors.

> "Unfortunately, [my room] was next the guests' kitchen, and the flues from the fires passing under it, I was baked in a temperature of 91°, although, in spite of warnings about tigers, the dangers from which are by no means imaginary, I kept both door and window open all night."[32]

By contrast, during that severely cold winter of 2000 – '01, my apartment's boiler refused to boil for several days, on several occasions. Thus there was no hot water for washing dishes nor for bathing; no ondol room heat, nothing to warm the hands or body in the bitter cold. The landlord said that the heat could not be fixed until the weather warmed, so I drove my car to Songtan, about four hours north, and stayed a few days with friends who had heat and a functional shower.

When I returned, the boiler was still not working. With the inside apartment temperature at 10° C (about 50° F), all I could think about was hot soup and a warm bed. I now have an existential understanding of the difference between 20° and 10° C as well as a personal awareness of the limits of homeothermy. While awake, I wore four or five layers of clothing (including a coat), and when I wanted to sleep at night, every blanket in my possession (including a sleeping bag) covered the bed.

Feeling so cold made it hard to concentrate on anything else, such as preparing lectures for classes. Doing laundry at the laundromat on base was a thermal reprieve. Finally, the UMUC office decided to put me up in billeting (on-base military housing) until the heater was fixed. At last, just before classes began on January 22, the heater was repaired, again after a threat of withholding rent by the Maryland housing coordinator, a Korean woman who helped enormously in dealing with this unreliable and often incompetent landlord who tried to blame the heating problems on me.

The Daewoo in snow, Taegu

Chapter 10

SOUTHERN COMFORT, KOREAN STYLE

While living in Taegu and teaching on bases there, I also had assignments in Pusan, a port on the southern coast of the peninsula, and in Kunsan, near its southwestern coast. To get to these teaching sites I traveled for several hours each way by bus or train, often gazing, enchanted, at the scenic Korean countryside.

For classes at Camp Hialeah in Pusan, I normally took the train into the city and then caught a cab to the base, although I drove the car back and forth from Taegu a few times to bring lab supplies from my apartment. It was normally a two to three hour trip one way, and I spent the night after class at billeting in Hialeah.

The trip from Taegu to Kunsan was much longer, more than five hours by bus, and required a change of buses. I was always afraid of missing the bus connection because the second bus didn't leave from a regular stall in the station. Rather, I had to decipher instructions in Korean on a board inside the station before I knew where to catch the second bus. Luckily, I never missed the connection. Once on the bus, I could relax and read or write or just enjoy the scenery.

The awesome scenery along the bus route across the central spine of Korean mountains inspired some of my most contemplative meditations on the country and its people. The bus drifted through a series of East Asian landscape paintings, creating in me a fondness verging on reverence for the Korean countryside. The city terminus of these trips, with the hustle and bustle and dirt, was always a jolt after passing through the idyllic hinterland.

One aspect of the mountainous Korean countryside that I particularly noticed during those bus rides was the appearance of the sun in the sky. The sun usually appeared white, with a fuzzy perimeter, rather than yellow or orange in color with a distinct rim, as I was used to seeing in the U.S. and Europe. I tried to figure out why the sun looked as it did. I have noticed in my travels throughout the world that the sun's aspect—an almost animate character as it casts light upon the land—is a feature that distinguishes one part of the globe from another.

In Korea, when the sun rose above the mountains in the morning, it was a brilliant, white, hazy sphere between or above the peaks, and because of the whiteness and the lack of a distinct circumference, it seemed brighter than the sun I was used to seeing at home. Some of the fuzziness was probably caused by the dense moisture in the air that blows in from the sea and across the Korean peninsula, to be captured as mist in the mountains. At some times of the year, particularly when rice fields were burned, a white smoke drifted lazily up from the fields and nestled in mountain crevices. This image evoked those hazy mountains scenes seen in Chinese landscape paintings.

I have since come to realize that the mist-shrouded Korean sun's apparent brilliance resulted from the fact that I was actually able to look at it for more than a fraction of a second without reflexively averting my eyes. In the U.S., I cannot even look at the sun except at sunrise or sunset, when its rays travel through a thick shield of atmosphere. Thus, I was able to appreciate a brilliant daytime sun in Korea because the atmospheric moisture and smoke offered sufficient protection for my retina that I was not forced to look away immediately.

J. A. V. Simson

In possession of a reasonably good vehicle that second year, I traveled to several fascinating sites not far from Taegu. Of course I went back to visit Kyongju (currently transliterated Gyeongju) and again marveled at tomb mounds and ancient artifacts of the Silla Kingdom. I also spent a day in Chinhae during its glorious cherry blossom festival, where I watched a whole pig roasting on a spit outdoors but wasn't able to sample it because it hadn't yet finished cooking.

Having become fairly confident and adventurous, I tried many different types of Korean food in sites around the southern part of the country, even at bus and train stations. Almost all Korean soups (*tang*) tasted quite good. Along with kim-chi, most food was served with a side of *ko-chu-chang*, an intensely hot, red-pepper paste; which is mixed with soup or other food to suit the taste. I developed a fondness for food on the hot (peppery) side—hotter than most Western food but not quite as hot as most Koreans prefer it. In the late summer and early fall, mats of drying red peppers were spread everywhere—alongside streets, beside homes, on patios and roof-tops. Everybody who had any kind of garden grew red peppers.

Red peppers are an important ingredient of Korea's signature food and favorite condiment, kim-chi. I never developed the fondness for it that Korean friends hoped I might, despite the fact that I ate a good deal of it. Kim-chi is eaten with almost every meal, and it probably helps with digestion and protects against bacteria.

At home in Songtan and Taegu, I usually cooked for myself—mostly with food purchased at the commissary on base. But on the road, either as a tourist or traveling to remote-site bases for teaching, I usually ate at local restaurants or bought "fast food" from road-side shops or street vendors. I always chose foods that were either cooked or pickled and never became ill from eating Korean food.

The tempuras—batter-covered, deep-fried fish, shrimp, and

vegetables—were always tasty. Another staple of road-side fast food was *kim-bap* (*gim-bap*), which looks much like Japanese sushi. Kim-bap consists of vegetables and rice rolled in algae leaves and then sliced into sections about half an inch thick. It sometimes contains cooked meat, but I never saw any with fish. I found it tastier than sushi, and there's no risk of eating uncooked meat or fish.

One of my favorite Korean dishes was *pajeon*, a type of pancake laced with green onions. It was delicious any time of the day, and I ate it anywhere I could find it. For larger meals in restaurants, if a Korean didn't accompany me and select the main course, I always chose *bulgogi*, sometimes called Mongolian beef. It is thinly sliced beef marinated in a sweet, tart, soy-barbeque sauce. It can be eaten alone or tucked into lettuce leaves along with rice and other vegetables.

There were a few food items in Korea that I tried but didn't like, such as fried silkworms, available in paper cones at outdoor festivals and considered a delicacy. A delicacy eaten by Koreans that I never tried was dog meat.

Near the end of the year in Taegu, I arranged a trip to Chejudo (now transliterated Jejudo, meaning 'ash island'). A volcanic island off the south-western coast of Korea, Chejudo is the Korean equivalent of Hawaii and a favorite honeymoon destination. I spent three days there and rented a car in order to be able to travel around the island comfortably. From almost anywhere on the island, I could see the central mountain, Hallasan, South Korea's highest peak. The volcano that formed the island is currently extinct.

The island's many holiday resort areas cater to special family events for those who live on the peninsula. In addition to its fine climate and semitropical foliage, tourists are drawn to amusement parks and casinos that dot the island. For me, these seriously detracted from the island's charm. Because I was there for only a long week-end, I didn't spend much time at the beaches or in tourist areas. One of the more appealing tourist destinations I visited on the island was the Yeomiji Botanical Gardens, a spacious structure enclosing a vast collection of local and exotic plants.

Littering the island are foamy lava-rocks that float. The islanders use these as building materials to construct fences and small buildings with thatched roofs. Pieces of lava are often carved into fanciful forms, including traditional small statues called *harubang*, little Korean gnomes with hats of a style found only on this island. These reminded me of miniature versions of Easter Island statuary.

Because of the favorable exchange rate between the Korean *won* and the American dollar, I could afford to travel to several countries in Asia and the Pacific much more cheaply than would have been possible from Japan. Places I visited while living in Korea included Thailand, China, Australia and Hawaii. But those are other stories.

Lava gnomes, Chejudo

SECTION III:

Reflections On The Korean Way

In the last few chapters of her book, *Korea and Her Neighbors*, Isabella Bishop reflected on her experiences of the Korean culture she encountered. In the following chapters, I also offer an overview of Korean culture as I experienced it, particularly as it has been influenced by events of the twentieth century. We were both interested in issues of religion and the roles of women. She was witness to the cultural chaos that accompanied the Japanese assault on Korean national autonomy in the late nineteenth century. I experienced the cultural tension of a peninsula divided between North and South, two countries with two utterly incompatible political philosophies.

Indeed, North and South Korea are still nominally at war, fifty years after the truce at Panmunjom, with both sides vying for control of the whole peninsula. Nonetheless, my positive impressions of Korea outweighed the negatives, which was true of Isabella Bishop as well. I was especially impressed by the energy and industry of the people of South Korea, and I admired their environmental savvy. A deep sadness continues to color my feelings for the people North of the DMZ.

Chapter 11

LANGUAGE, CLASS, AND CULTURE

Annyong hasseyo? means 'Are you at peace?' It is the standard greeting in Korea—rather like 'How are you?' in English. The standard answer is *Ne, hasseyo?* meaning, 'Yes, are you?' A more formal rendering of this standard greeting, and one that's often given in Korean phrase books but rarely encountered on the street, is *Annyong hasshimnika?* This means the same thing, except that one is asking the question in a more formal and deferential way. This form of greeting is given in many tourist phrase books, probably so that foreigners saying it will appear as polite as possible to Koreans. There are at least three other verb forms of this greeting that reflect the different respect levels characterizing Korean social discourse.

The problem for the foreigner is that she would like to learn just *one* language, not two or more, in order to communicate. For example, at least five verb levels reflect different degrees of formality, respect and/or friendship. Also, the subject of the sentence may require a respectful form of the verb (often with a different root) if it involves a dignitary or one's ancestors. Any moderately fluent Korean speaker can switch among the respect levels with ease in a mixed social setting, the way Swiss can switch between German, French and Italian in ordinary dinner conversation with guests from different parts of the country. The nearest comparable construct Westerners are exposed to in a European language is the distinction between the familiar versus the formal second person pronoun and verb forms (*e.g.*, French *tu* and *vous;* German *du* and *Sie*).

This multiple respect level of verb construction is one of the most difficult aspects of the Korean language for a Westerner to master, which is part of the reason I never felt comfortable speaking Korean. Maneuvering the linguistic maze reflects a basic aspect of Korean cultural history, which has been dominated by Confucian culture for a millennium. Korean culture practiced an even more strictly hierarchical social structure than did either China or Japan, with all access to learning being hereditary. Honor, respect and hierarchical relationships form the cornerstones of Confucian culture; they have contributed to the stability of Confucian societies for millennia.

The yangban, who constituted the upper class in Yi-dynasty Korea, controlled both education and the political apparatus of the country. Education and writing systems followed Chinese models, although Korean practices were probably more rigid. The lower classes generally had little or no education and were culturally and linguistically distinct from the upper class. This was also true in feudal Europe to some extent. The educated yangban upper class always used a "high" level of language with honorific verb and noun forms, as well as many Chinese loan words, including numbers, whereas the lower classes used mostly native Korean vocabulary. Thus, it would be easy for a native to tell whether a person was of the upper or lower class by speech patterns.

Such was the basis of the social structure when Isabella Bishop arrived in Korea, and she deplored the yangban control over Korean culture. She saw the educated officials as effete and lazy (scholars didn't work for a living), social parasites on the laboring lower classes. In a chapter entitled: "Education and Foreign Trade," she declared at the outset, *"Korean education has hitherto failed to produce patriots, thinkers or honest men."*[33] Although they were educated as Confucian scholars and held all official positions, the yangban officials apparently did not receive the type of training that encouraged a strong moral impetus for justice or duty. She wrote:

> *"Narrowness, grooviness, conceit, superciliousness, a false pride which despises manual labor, a selfish individualism, destructive of generous public spirit and social trustfulness, a slavery in act and thought to customs and traditions 2,000 years old, a narrow intellectual view, a shallow moral sense, and an estimate of women essentially degrading, appear to be the products of the Korean educational system."*[34]

The yangban men she contacted were largely loungers and sneerers at the local yamens (government buildings) or in town squares during her travels in the countryside. It does not appear that she had much conversation with any of them. They probably would not have deigned to speak with her. Her servants and translators were not yangban, and their mistrust of the upper class may have contributed to her negative opinions.

The yangban class no longer exists, at least not officially, and a Confucian education is no longer required of bureaucrats. Still, honorifics persist in the Korean language and color the culture. The different respect levels in all parts of the language (verb and noun forms, as well as titles) contribute to its difficulty for the foreigner. One must learn multiple forms of a verb or a noun so as to express the level of respect one holds toward both the listener and the subject of a sentence. The respect levels and other major differences in grammatical constructs make Korean, like other Asian languages, particularly challenging for Westerners.

Of course the Korean language has a grammar, but it is *not* much like Indo-European grammar. Yes, there are subjects and predicates, but that's about the extent of grammatical similarity. Modifying and relational words as used in English (e.g., adjectives, adverbs and prepositions) are largely indicated by endings (postpositions) added to nouns, or by syllables inserted at the beginning or into the middle of verbs and nouns.

Korean is generally considered an Ural-Altaic language (like Mongolian, Turkic, and Hungarian) although it is now lumped into a separate category with Japanese and Ainu. It seems to have come out of the high central Asian plateau, as did the Korean people themselves. Thus, there are very few Korean words with English or Indo-European cognates. And Korean has a linguistic structure that is almost as daunting to a non-native speaker as is English. Today, very few people—except Koreans and American military intelligence officers—bother to learn the Korean alphabet or the language itself. This is a shame because the alphabet is very easy to learn.

Many Western businessmen learn either Japanese or Chinese so as to take advantage of emerging business opportunities in these countries. Japan was occupied and then economically rehabilitated by the U.S. and its allies after World War II, as was Germany. Since then, Japan has become economically strong and Japanese is an important language of trade. China has the largest population of any Asian nation and has exploded as a trading nation. Many people in Asia (including Russians) study Chinese. It has even become a language to learn in the West, although largely in its spoken form.

By contrast, Korea was battered and exploited for half a century, not by nuclear attack but by the depredations of Japanese occupation followed by the Korean War. And then it was left largely to its own devices for economic rehabilitation. Despite everything, the country has made enormous economic strides, but not so much that being able to speak Korean confers an advantage on businessmen of other nationalities. Few are motivated by the challenge alone if the payoff is so slim. As a consequence, Koreans have unfortunately made almost no literary—and only minor technical—impact on world culture. This is regrettable because, when translated well, Korean literature can express poignancy and insight rivaling anything one might find in other Asian literatures.[35]

The Korean language as now written has a unique script, the Hangul alphabet, originally designed under the patronage of King Sejong the Great in the 15th century. This script was termed *En-mun* by Isabella Bishop wherever she referred to the common Korean script in her narrative. The Hangul alphabet is strictly phonetic and is much easier to learn and read than either Japanese or Chinese. It has only a few more sound symbols than the Latin alphabet, and it uses simple pen or brush strokes for letters, arranged in block-like syllables. These syllables are the basic meaning units of words. Each word root is usually composed of one to three syllables. Because it is so much easier to learn Hangul than the Chinese script, which employs thousands of distinct word characters, Hangul was used for years in Korea mostly by court ladies and merchants. The upper-class scholars, whose lifetime business was learning, preferred the pretentiousness of the infinitely more difficult Chinese script. Even today, Chinese script (*hanja*) may be seen on shop signs, denoting a merchant who hopes to attract a high-class clientele.

The Hangul alphabet did not come into wide usage in Korea until the latter half of the twentieth century. Prior to the twentieth century, it was considered a low-class alphabet and was disdained by cultured yangban. During the first half of the twentieth century in Japanese-occupied Korea, the Korean language was discouraged, and its script was forbidden. Koreans were given Japanese names, and school classes were taught mostly in Japanese. After liberation, Koreans began to use the native Hangul script almost universally, as a way to reassert national, cultural autonomy.

Some members of the yangban class collaborated with Japanese occupiers in the first half of the twentieth century; hence there is some mistrust of the upper class language. Not surprisingly, a bit of cultural and linguistic schizophrenia surrounds the whole language issue. Nonetheless, the most polite forms of the language (e.g., . . .*mnida* and. . .*mnika* verb endings) are used in public announcements, but these are rarely encountered on the street.

For all of Bishop's contempt for the yangban, they greatly valued education, and that high regard for education prevails in contemporary Korean culture. Moreover, the yangban, who may have siphoned off much productivity of the lower classes during the later Yi-dynasty period, did not have the riches, nor exhibit the ostentation that we in the West have come to associate with aristocracy. Though educated and steeped in Confucian hierarchical values, many yangban were country farmers.

During my second year in Korea, I audited a Korean language course, took all the tests and did well, but didn't have much chance to use the language on a daily basis. I taught in English, and most of my social interactions were with UMUC faculty and staff, also in English. Despite some proficiency in several languages, I was never able to learn more than the rudiments of Korean. In the end, I became frustrated with—even ashamed of—my failure to catch on to it. Once, when I told a colleague I intended to learn Korean, he said to me, "If you go through that desert, you will discover the bones of many who have gone there before you." Now my bones are strewn among them.

The few Americans I knew there who had some Korean proficiency had Korean wives or lovers, but even they (military linguists excepted) usually stumbled and struggled through anything but perfunctory exchanges with Koreans. And they were often met with good-natured ridicule by Korean friends and acquaintances while trying to converse.

A Korean woman, who lived not far from my apartment in Taegu, offered to speak Korean with me if I would help her with English. Mrs. Kim, mentioned in a previous chapter, wanted to learn

English as much I wanted to learn Korean, and our facilities with each other's languages were probably equivalent. I had had a year of struggling to learn Korean, and she had probably had a few years of poorly taught English in school. So twice a week I visited her shop, where we would drink tea and, with the best of intentions, try to have a conversation.

Usually the conversation would begin in Korean, then switch to English, and then back, both of us looking for words in our respective dictionaries or reading through lesson books we might have at hand. We became friends, and she was very helpful in some of my dealings with local merchants. We even did some countryside touring together. But our misunderstandings were numerous, and I only vaguely understood what her situation was, although she was clearly a woman of substance.

One misunderstanding was a source of grief to both of us. It concerned my telephone as I was preparing to leave the country. The Koreans (or at least Mrs. Kim) used the phrase 'call me' to mean 'the telephone,' perhaps because the Korean verb 'to telephone' is translated as 'to call' in Korean-English dictionaries. Mrs. Kim had wanted me to give her my phone when I left, and I would have done so willingly. "Call me when you go," she said.

The problem was that I thought she wanted me to phone her before I left, which I did. She came over just as I was about to leave the apartment, and the phone was gone. One of the movers had talked me out of it and I saw no reason not to give it to him. I had been giving away appliances, books, and clothing for the previous two weeks in order to lessen the burden of transport back to the U.S. Finally, after exclamations and gestures, I realized what she had wanted, but it was too late. With some more prodding, it became clear that she really wanted the long extension cord for the phone, so I went to base and bought one for her at the BX. But we both felt vaguely defeated about the incident.

J. A. V. Simson

When answering the phone, one says: *Yoboseyo*, which means roughly 'Hey there.' That term can also be used to address a stranger if help is needed urgently. However, it's important to be careful about how and with whom that term is used because it is also the way men address their wives—or so I was told by a reliable Korean—and the phrase can carry overtones of either affection or disrespect.

The following are a few hints for learning—and using—enough of the language to enhance the pleasure of a trip to this marvelous little country. First of all, learning the alphabet is essential, and that's not difficult. However, in the Hangul alphabet, it's important to realize that single letters don't stand alone in written Korean. Rather, letters are arranged in block-like syllables, in which letters are written from left to right and top to bottom in a standard form for a given syllable. Each letter is adjusted in size to fit within the block. For example, 한 is the root of the number 'one' and is pronounced 'han' with ㅎ being the 'h' sound; ㅏ being the 'a' sound; and ㄴ being the 'n' sound. Together, they are written as the syllable, 한. Koreans are justly proud of the esthetic appeal of a well constructed block syllable.

Each syllable is itself a meaning unit, and most are words whose meanings you can look up in a dictionary. To form words and sentences, the block syllables (rather than individual letters) may be written either from left to right, as in most books and newspapers, or from top to bottom, as in many shop signs. Most words are compound words, and if you know the meaning of the single elements (syllables), you can often figure out the meaning of the word. In pronouncing a Korean word, the syllables are usually all given equal emphasis, unlike in English, where syllabic stress can determine meaning. However, questions do have rising end syllables.

For example, *Hana* indicates the number 'one.' Koreans consider themselves the Han people, and their country is *Hanguk*, the country

Korea, Are You at Peace?

of the Han. Thus, Hanguk (Korea) is the one (main) country or the first country or the country of the first people. It's pretty easy to guess that the syllable for country is *guk* or *kuk*. *Miguk* means America, or the U.S. *Mi* can also mean beauty, so Miguk can mean beautiful country. Chinese also uses the word 'Han' to mean original people, although 'Han' is not the root for 'one' in Chinese.[36] The word *saram* also means 'people,' so Koreans are *Hanguksaram*.

Some common syllables encountered in tourist destinations include *Puk, Nam, Tong,* and *So,* the points of the compass: North, South, East and West. *Mun* is 'gate,' so *Nammun* means south gate. *Tae* (or *dae*) is 'great,' so *Taemun* is 'great gate' or portal. And *Namdaemun* would be 'Great South Gate.' *Sa* means 'temple,' so Pulguksa is 'Pulguk Temple' (or temple of the country of fire). Other syllables commonly encountered in place names are *do* – region, province or island; *gang* – river; and *san* – mountain. Hence, Hangang is the Han River, which flows through Seoul and enters the Yellow Sea near the border between North and South Korea; Chejudo, is a volcanic island, Cheju Island, or Ash Island; and Soraksan means Mount Sorak.

Unfortunately, it is often difficult to transliterate Korean letters and sounds into English, as conventions are not truly standardized. This became clear to me when I encountered the many unfamiliar transliterations in Isabella Bishop's book, where, for example, she speaks of 'Fusan' whereas today it would be written Pusan or Busan. Transliterations for the sounds 'l' and 'r' can be interchanged, as can 'f' and 'p,' or 'k' and 'g,' or 'd' and 't,' or 'j' and 'ch,' or 'p' and 'b' (or even 'v'). The letter that is written as 'g' or 'k' (as in the syllable *kuk* or *guk*) will often be transliterated as 'k' at the beginning of a word but as 'g' in the middle of a word because within a word the sound is softened and vocalized. Moreover, whenever an 's' is followed by an 'i,' the 's' is softened to 'sh.' Thus, the ancient kingdom, whose capital was at Kyongju, is sometimes transliterated as 'Silla' and

111

sometimes as 'Shilla'. Thus, it's necessary to be flexible and try multiple transliterations when looking up a word in the dictionary. Recent efforts to standardize transliterations ("romanizations") of Korean words, particularly place names, have resulted in accepted spellings quite different than those in use when I was in Korea. I have included a list of common words and place names used in this narrative, now often spelled differently in English, on p. 165 following the Appendix.

With regard to Korean names, the surname, or family name is always placed first, and the common or familiar name, usually two syllables, is placed after the surname when referring to a person. Thus, Kim Il-sung would be westernized to Il-sung Kim. However, when speaking with a Korean, *always* use the family name, **not** the familiar name. The conventions for writing names in Western script are not consistent. For example both Kim Il Sung and Kim Il-sung are acceptable versions. Kim is probably the most common Korean family name. Two other names frequently encountered are: Yi (or Lee) and Pak (often transliterated 'Park'). Other Korean names such as Choe, Im, Chang, Chon, Chung and Min are also common; some may be of Chinese origin.

When addressing a Korean, you should always use the family name followed by an honorific—most commonly *son saeng nim*, meaning 'most honorable' or 'teacher.' Among Korean adults, the familiar name is almost never used unless they have grown up together as children. Mrs. Kim and I always addressed each other by our last names. I can still sometimes hear an echo of her calling outside my door, *"Sim-son."*

Anyone planning a visit to Korea should at least try to learn the alphabet. It is easy and will allow you to read signs. Take a dictionary with you at all times. If possible, try to use the language with locals. And graciously accept any help offered in English. I found most Koreans, especially women, to be almost infinitely patient with my awkward attempts to communicate, and most friendly and generous if I was respectful. A smile and a bow (hands held as if in prayer, with a slight forward tilt of the head) can certainly facilitate personal communication in Korea.

Yangban country village

Chapter 12

RELIGION, BELIEF, AND HOPE

I spent Christmas in my apartment in Songtan that first year in Korea. A light snow powdered the ground and the nearby roofs visible through sliding glass doors of the back balcony. Korea normally has very little snow in winter, but that year I had a white Christmas halfway around the globe from home.

Although about a third of the inhabitants of South Korea are nominally Christians, they don't herald Christmas with bright, gaudy displays or loud, repetitive music as is common in the U.S. Many Americans I knew in Korea missed the Christmas spectacle. Even on base, only a few Christmas trees, modest in size, graced key officers' buildings. Koreans, who struggled for years to reforest their mountains after a half century of ecological disaster from war and want, would no doubt have been outraged if many healthy trees had been killed so frivolously. Koreans retain a reverence for the natural world that is part of their religious heritage.

Religion and ethics in Korea are an amalgam, a unique mix of multiple religious traditions that have percolated down to the present from the past—including the prehistoric past. Such a fusion of religious influences and practices is termed syncretism and is perhaps nowhere more evident than in Korea. Koreans do not look to any codified version of their religious beliefs; rather, religious practices form the substratum of their understanding of the world and the expression of their spiritual life.

Isabella Bishop usually labeled the native religion of Korea "daemon worship" or "daemonism" throughout her narrative, and she devoted two chapters to the prevalent mystical folk practices of the time. In a chapter titled "Daemonism or Shamanism," she described the external trappings of this mystical system, of which she says, *"I dare not call it a religion."*[37] She found the practices grotesque and the influence on the psyche of the people injurious.

In her explanation, there were two types of shamans: *Pan-su* (blind wizards, male) and *mu-tang* (usually female shamans). Isabella consistently capitalized Pan-su, but wrote mu-tang in lower case. (This might be a glimpse of sexism in a woman who tried to *"live...a life fit for a man."*[38]) According to her descriptions of their different functions, Pan-su controlled the myriad surrounding spirits by incantations and formulae, were especially important as geomancers in determining the location of houses and graves, and were also actively involved in divination and casting horoscopes.

By contrast, in the chapter titled "Notes on Daemonism Concluded," she expanded on the function of the mu-tang, usually considered to be possessed by a familiar spirit. Through the medium of this spirit, coupled with ritualistic dancing, the mu-tang propitiated malevolent spirits and helped bring about a client's desired outcome. Queen Min, the last Korean queen, apparently employed a mu-tang in her efforts to become pregnant with a son and to produce an heir to the Korean throne. The spell seemed to work, but the fates of both mother and son were ultimately tragic, as the mother was murdered and the son eventually became a puppet monarch under Japanese control.

Bishop also included a short laundry list of various types of spirits that might be encountered in the daily life of Koreans and that might be influenced by the arts and practices of shamans. In her consideration of Korean religion, she concludes:

> "The Koreans, it must be remarked, have no single word for Daemonism or Shamanism. The only phrase in use to express their belief in daemons who require to be propitiated is, Kursin wi han-nan Kot (the worship of Spirits). Pulto is Buddhism, Yuto Confucianism, and Sonto Taoism, but the termination To, "doctrine," has not yet been affixed to Daemonism."[39]

During her trek through the Diamond Mountains in the northeastern part of the Korean peninsula, Isabella stayed in Buddhist monasteries instead of village inns. She remarked on the mixed iconography—images of Buddhist, Hindu, and shamanistic symbols interwoven in temple wall paintings. She considered Buddhism moribund and the monks grossly ignorant and superstitious, chanting phrases whose meanings they did not understand. Still, she found them pleasant and hospitable, and much better hosts than the contemptuous and lazy upper-class yangban she encountered in villages and cities outside these mountain retreats.

Bishop scarcely wrote about Taoism in Korea; she may not have recognized it as separate from animism or Shamanism. And she had almost universal contempt for the influence of Confucianism, particularly the oppressive class structure it codified. It should be remembered that Isabella Lucy Bird Bishop was a preacher's daughter. One of her major support systems while in Korea was a network of Protestant missionaries, particularly Presbyterian, established throughout the peninsula.

Following comments on an exorcism in her book, Bishop also discussed the on-going Christian mission work in Korea. This had gained momentum in *"Phyong-yang"* after its destruction by the Chinese and Japanese in the war she had recently fled. Missionaries, the most successful of which were Americans, brought medical supplies and educational opportunities along with theology. Hope was sustained in these missions subsequently during the long half-century of Japanese occupation following Isabella Bishop's departure. Given the extent of missionary work she described, it is not surprising that such a high proportion of the current Korean population is Christian.

The following is a brief overview of the major religious influences and practices in the Korean peninsula, derived not only from my personal experiences, but also from conversations and readings.[40] These religious influences include: nature worship, Shamanism, Taoism, Buddhism, Confucianism, and Christianity.

Nature worship, or animism, has its basis in the notion that all natural objects, both animate and inanimate—including rocks, mountains, trees, and animals—contain spirits that are inherent to their being and behavior. According to Webster's New Universal Unabridged Dictionary, animism is: "The belief that natural phenomena and objects such as rocks, trees, the wind, etc., are alive and have souls."[41] This is probably the most fundamental type of human religious belief, and it persists to the present in the form of totems, talismans, and everyday notions (often termed superstitions) of even the most culturally advanced peoples.

Shamanism (*Mu-sok*) is based on early folk beliefs in the multiplicity of spirits, many of them malevolent, which can affect people's lives and can be controlled to some extent by individuals (shamans) who have special spiritual power. It is still practiced on the Korean peninsula, and forms the core of many traditional ceremonies, especially dances, relating to local and national holidays. It also permeates activities surrounding special events in individual lives. Determining sites and times of burial, wedding dates and partners, the orientation of houses and room furniture, and many special ceremonies involve the services of geomancers (shamans), comparable to the Chinese practice of feng-shui.

The belief that spirits of good and evil can be controlled by especially gifted and trained individuals (*e.g.,* shamans or witch doctors) is found in many cultures. But its elevation to the status of national cultural icon is found only in Korea. Intervention on behalf of individuals or groups usually takes the form of trances and dances by a shaman or a troupe of shamanistic dancers. Of particular cultural significance is the fact that many Korean shamans are women (mutang), an important pathway to respect and power in an otherwise male dominated culture.

Animistic and shamanistic beliefs and practices in Korea probably arose in north-central Asia, among the Tungus peoples. These practices are especially prevalent in northeastern Asia as they also are among Native Americans. Such shamanistic practices no doubt accompanied the eastward migration of Tungusic ancestors of Amerindians across the Bering Straits into the Western Hemisphere during the late Paleolithic period.

In her book *Korea's Cultural Roots*,[42] Jon Carter Covell found the symbols of Shamanism and Taoism much more culturally interesting than did Isabella Bishop. Indeed, Covell has called Shamanism "the mother-matrix" for the common people of the Korean peninsula. Likewise, David Mason, in *Spirit of the Mountains*,[43] sympathetically described the religious roots of sacred symbolism surrounding the mountain spirit (San-shin) as derived from both Shamanism and Taoism (also written Daoism).

The primary goal of shamanistic practices is to protect individuals and communities from capricious and malevolent spirits (demons), which can cause disease and misfortune. The shaman's aim is to ensure long life and good fortune for his/her clients. Koreans freely admit that Shamanism underlies many of their traditional folk customs and art, particularly dance, music and theater. There is a frank chapter on Shamanism in *Korean Heritage II*[44] by the Korean Overseas Information Service that emphasizes the central role of shamanistic beliefs and practices to Korean culture. Moreover, Buddhism, as it is practiced in Korea, includes many elements of Shamanism, and shamanistic symbols decorate most Buddhist temples.

Taoism *(Sonto)*, 'The Way,' arrived from China in the first millennium C.E. and has become interwoven with both shamanistic and Buddhist practices in Korea. While never adopted as an official religion, Taoism has had a major influence on the native nature worship, particularly as related to geomancy and the reverence for mountains and rocks. Taoism does not figure heavily in most considerations of Korean religious history, although Covell considers Buddhism, Shamanism, Neo-Confucianism, and Taoism the major roots of Korean cultural history.[45] Mason considers Taoism the source of the geomancy which has been (and still is) integral to decision-making regarding holy places, graves, wedding sites, etc.[46] Also, the South Korean flag is clearly based on Taoist symbology. Korean beliefs and practices are, indeed, syncretistic.

Buddhism *(Pulto)* first arrived in Korea during the fourth century C.E. and became the national religion of Koguryo, one of the Three Kingdoms of that period. From there it spread to Paekche and then to Silla and became the national religion when the Silla Kingdom united most of the peninsula under one dynasty. The subsequent rulers of Koryo also embraced Buddhism, but eventually the interference of Buddhist monks in politics led to anti-Buddhist sentiment among Korean rulers. With the fall of Koryo and the rise of the Choson Kingdom (Yi dynasty, 1392 – 1905), Buddhism regained some political tolerance, but an undercurrent of anti-Buddhist sentiment has persisted, underscored by caricatures of monks in Korean folk plays. As it is practiced, Korean Buddhism retains a strong shamanistic flavor.

At a Buddhist temple restaurant in Seoul during our first week in Korea, new faculty recruits were treated to a Korean folk dance.

This dance, of which I subsequently saw several versions—including one at the Korean Folk Village—was clearly shamanistic. The dances included women in flowing robes, brilliantly colored long scarves billowing from their arms, twirling, bowing, and rising in some pre-set ritualistic pattern to the whining music and frenzied drumming of folk instruments.

Buddhist temples are among the most valuable traditional buildings and cultural artifacts that survived the devastations of 20th century Korea. They are currently treated with great respect and reverence. The beautiful temple roofs and eaves are usually kept well tiled and painted, and the temples and grounds are cared for by monks who live there. Shrines and temple complexes are visited by tourists as well as by local adherents who perform the simple, quiet rituals expected during visits to the temples. Busloads of schoolchildren visit temples on field trips, and so receive a taste of the cultural faith and esthetic that dominated the country for so much of its history.

Confucianism *(Yuto)*, while not addressing the supernatural domain, has fulfilled many religious functions in eastern Asia, including Korea. Some might not consider Confucianism a religion at all because it does not include a concept of God in its tenets. But neither does Buddhism, although the latter deals extensively with the spiritual realm. However, if one views religion as a set of stories and beliefs about the nature of the world, which beliefs are ethically determinative, then Confucianism can be considered a religion. Confucianism probably entered Korea from China through Koguryo during the Three Kingdoms period (roughly 100 B.C.E. to 650 C.E.). As a moral force directing the behavior of individuals as well as of governmental institutions, its influence extended throughout the Koryo Kingdom and into the Yi Dynasty. During the more than five centuries of that dynasty, Korean Confucianism directed the avowed ethics of the yangban upper class.

Upper-class males were educated in Confucian academies in preparation for service to their families, their communities, and their country. Training in the Confucian classics taught respect, loyalty, honor, and discipline, as well as protocol and behavioral rituals. The assumptions of the system were highly hierarchical; age, high social status, and education were accorded the greatest respect. Males had unquestioned authority over females, who were seldom allowed out of their home compounds, particularly among the upper classes. By the late nineteenth century, Confucian practices had become stylized, reactionary and dysfunctional; the ideal of service had deteriorated into a sense of entitlement. As noted earlier, Isabella Bishop had little respect for the Confucian-trained yangban officials she encountered during her travels in Korea, as this training produced primarily an assumption of privilege.

Christianity entered Korea in the very recent history of the peninsula, but it has taken greater hold there than in any other Asian country. It began with the introduction of Catholicism in the late 18th century by a Korean scholar, Yi Sung-hun, who had been baptized in Peking. Christianity was termed *Sohak* or 'Western Learning,' and continued to attract adherents until active persecution became official policy in the late 19th century. In the meantime, Protestant missionaries, many from America, began to establish schools and hospitals; these were viewed positively, given Korean respect for education. Girls were also educated in the missionary schools. It was through missionary contacts that Isabella Bishop obtained much of her assistance during her travels. By some estimates, nearly half of contemporary Koreans who profess a religious faith claim to be Christians.

The appeal of Christianity is rather difficult to understand in this otherwise highly traditional culture. It may have partly to do with the lack of an official religion at the time that Christianity entered Korea. Confucianism does not claim to deal with the spiritual dimension of human experience, other than in terms of inter-personal relationships and respectful behavior. Two other factors were probably more important in the success of Korean Christianity.

For one thing, Christian missionaries established schools and hospitals very early after their arrival, and they ministered to the needs of the population with food, education and health care during a Korean regime that had become so corrupt and parasitic that the general population was left with no support and few resources. Those schools and hospitals impressed Koreans who experienced the benefits of this Western Learning.

Secondly, during the Japanese occupation of the early twentieth century, many of those who led Korean nationalist movements and who resisted the Japanese imposition of Shinto worship, had been educated in Christian schools. Moreover, several Christian ministers and missionaries were killed by Japanese for trying to protect their Korean flock, becoming martyrs in the eyes of many. Such self-sacrifice elevated Christianity in the esteem of Koreans living through those difficult times. The burning of Christian churches during the Japanese occupation was achingly rendered by Pearl S. Buck in *Living Reed, A Novel of Korea*.[47]

It could also be that the active, dynamic character of Christianity, contrasting with the passive nature of Buddhism and the rigidity of Confucianism, accounts for some of the appeal of Christianity for Koreans, who are generally active, dynamic people.

A major feature of the night cityscape in any Korean town, large or small, is its forest of illuminated red crosses that rise above the dark, angular urban silhouette. The architecture of Christian churches in Korea is unlike that of Western churches, whether European, Slavic or American. Korean churches are often high, box-like buildings lacking the graceful domes and arches, towers and steeples of Western churches, but they serve the esthetics of those who constructed them.

Of the Koreans with whom I became friendly enough to speak of religion, their belief systems spanned the gamut of all those mentioned above. One woman who worked at the UMUC office at the Osan airbase was married to an American ex-serviceman and was nominally a Christian, but she was also quite superstitious and probably held many shamanistic beliefs. Another woman who befriended me in Songtan originally came to my door as a Jehovah's Witness. We spent many a Saturday afternoon discussing religion and beliefs; we also shared food and life stories. A Korean man, who was a faculty member with the University of Maryland and had spent many years in the U.S., was clearly of yangban origin and spoke a great deal about Confucian principles and practices as he had learned them in school. My best friend in Taegu was a Buddhist, and she took me to several Buddhist temples in the vicinity of the city. Neither of us knew the other's language well enough to discuss religion, but she participated in rituals at the temples and tried to explain some of them to me without much success. I didn't know any avowed shamanists, although for a time there was a store-front organization near my apartment in Taegu where much chanting went on at certain times of the day and evening. I suspected it was a shamanistic organization, although the attendees all seemed to be males.

The rich religious and cultural stew that emerges from this highly diverse combination of influences is uniquely Korean. A sedate and peaceful Buddhist affect, combined with an orderly, stylized Confucian demeanor, and tempered by Christian devotion and social consciousness, collectively form the veneer of the culture. This respectable cultural surface may erupt periodically with frenzied shamanistic dances and wailing instruments, voices of the deep Korean past projected forward into our time.

Buddhist monk at Pulguksa

Chapter 13

WOMEN IN KOREA

"I married an American because I never wanted to have to obey—or even listen to—another *otoshe*. They don't know anything. But you have to pay attention to them and do what they say anyway." So said a woman sitting next to me on a bus from Camp Long to Kimpo Airport. In Korean, *otoshe* means 'uncle' and is used generically for an older Korean man; the female equivalent, *ajuma*, means 'auntie.'

My seat-mate, originally Korean, then elaborated on relationships between men and women in Korea. She described how she had escaped a typical Korean marriage by marrying an American G.I. She said her choice of husband had poisoned her relationship with her Korean family. Koreans do not consider anyone who is not Korean— particularly an American soldier—to be a good marriage choice for a daughter. After she and her husband had lived for several years in the U.S., he had generously volunteered for another tour of duty in Korea so she could care for her aging mother who was ill. Her mother had welcomed her back into the family and had reluctantly accepted her husband.

After about a year in Korea, I had formed an idea of the subculture of Korean women that didn't change much during the following year. Despite outward appearances of Western-style modernization, Korea is still a Confucian culture with its respect for age and the importance of education. Less appealing aspects of traditional Asian cultures include a reverence for the past (ancestors and traditions) that verges on idolatry and an intensely hierarchical social structure with a strong gender bias favoring males. This leaves females, particularly young females, at the bottom of the social ladder.

In the past, women were generally confined to the family compound, a walled enclosure shielded from entry and view against those outside the family. Women could not go out or even see outside the compound. This was particularly true of women of the yangban class when Isabella Bishop was in Korea A piece of leisure equipment, the bouncing board, was used primarily by women in play and recreation inside their compounds. It was a long, flexible board attached at both ends to elevated struts, and women could stand on it and bounce up and down, as on a trampoline. It is widely claimed that this was a favorite form of entertainment for women because, if they bounced high enough, they could see what was happening outside the compound walls. Lower-class women were allowed out of the family compound and went into the fields to help with the farming. They were also servants in yangban homes and hence had some exposure to the outside world.

In *Korea and Her Neighbors,* Bishop included a chapter entitled "The Social Position of Women." In this chapter she elaborated on the inequality of women that was hardly less conspicuous than the inequality between the yangban and the peasant farmers she encountered in her daily travels. She also sprinkled remarks about women and their toil throughout her book. In an early chapter recounting her arrival in Seoul, she briefly described two categories of women: (1) poor servant women who could go out by day, primarily to perform menial tasks such as laundry and (2) more respectable women who were only permitted out at night, from eight o'clock until midnight, at which time men were banned from the streets.

Women were then allowed to wander the streets, accompanied by servants carrying lanterns. She claimed that Korean women were very rigidly secluded, perhaps more than women of any other nation she had visited.

Throughout her book, when describing stopovers in Korean villages, she commented on the rude curiosity of women of the lower classes. She also mentioned their toil, including the constant laundering of men's white linen garments, which required beating on riverside stones, treatment with lye, sun bleaching, beating with wooden paddles, and stiffening with a rice starch.

> *"The peasant woman may be said to have no pleasures. She is nothing but a drudge, till she can transfer some of the drudgery to her daughter-in-law. At thirty she looks fifty, and at forty is frequently toothless."*[48]

She was less able to describe the life of upper class women, inasmuch as they were absolutely secluded in the family compound. They emerged from their compounds in the city only at night, in a rigidly enclosed chaise.

> *"The seclusion of women was introduced five centuries ago by the present dynasty, in a time of great social corruption, for the protection of the family, and has probably continued, not. . .because men distrust their wives, but because they distrust each other, and with good reason, for the immorality of the cities and of the upper classes almost exceeds belief. Thus all young women, and all older women except those of the lowest class, are secluded within the inner courts of the houses by a custom which has more than the force of law."*[49]

She also described the Korean *gesang* (now written *kisaeng*) who were very similar in training and skills to Japanese geishas.

The words are similar enough that they probably have a common etymology. She had the opportunity to receive gesang and observed their well dressed grace and their dancing skill. She claimed that a difference between Japanese geishas and Korean gesang was that the latter were never taken as wives by respectable (Korean) men.

Even today, women in Korea are considered socially inferior and are generally expected to live under the protection of a male: father, husband, older son, or even brother. Nonetheless, the lifestyles and choices of younger Korean women are changing rapidly. A compelling set of recently published short stories entitled *Wayfarer, New Fiction by Korean Women*[50] allows a glimpse into the contemporary existential anguish of Korean women peering into a dark chasm separating traditional and modern Korean cultures.

As in all societies in which the role of women changes with industrialization and diminished family size, a cultural dissonance has arisen as women take on new roles in the society, but their traditional roles remain embedded in family traditions and in their psyches. Korean women often feel insecure, socially marginalized, and dissatisfied with their status and life choices. The recent election of a woman, Park Geun-hye, as president of South Korea reflected as powerful a cultural shift in that country as did the election of Barack Obama as president of the United States. Her insecure and inexperienced North Korean counterpart, Kim Jung-un, may consider that a woman in the president's office indicates weakness in the South. Does he view this as an opportunity to use force as a solution to the long-standing two-state problem? Let us hope not.

Despite their inferior social status, most Korean women I met were lively and good-natured. And like Korean men, they were usually strong-willed—all excellent qualities in people of a country that has had to rebuild itself after more than a half century of destruction and chaos.

Korea, Are You at Peace?

One source of strength and optimism among Korean women is the support and friendship of other women. No matter that the men have the power in the family, that they need to be served and catered to and can do as they wish; the women have each other, and get together for tea and endless gossip in one another's homes, go shopping together often, and laugh heartily amongst themselves. I had the sense that some of that laughter between women involved making fun of absent husbands.

A friend recently mentioned the phenomenal success of Korean women in international golf tournaments. Golf is a favorite Korean sport; golf cages (huge, netted enclosures) dot the Korean landscape and can even be found in cities. Whenever I would drive by one, or pass by on a train or bus, these golf cages were full of men and women practicing their game. In golf, Korean women may have found an honorable pathway to fame and fortune.

Traditionally, some women had power in Korean shamanistic rituals as mutang (priestesses). In a chapter entitled "Exorcists and Dancing Women," Isabella Bishop described an exorcism with its drum-beating accompaniment to the dancing female shaman in her flowing robes and silk scarves and trailers, executing the whirling traditional dance—part performance and part sorcery—intended to bring about some desired result. This type of dance by a mutang was termed a *kut* by Jon Carter Covell[51] in her sympathetic treatment of Korean Shamanism.

In shamanistic rituals, women are as likely as men to have power over the spirits. This may have given Korean women an internalized sense of potential power and importance. Also, women have had to cope and make lives for themselves and their families when their husbands were deported, as happened under the Japanese occupation, and when husbands were killed, as happened during the Korean War. When women are forced to take control of their own lives and the lives of others, it becomes a habit that is difficult to break, even in a strongly patriarchal society.

During the year I lived in Osan, one of the three Korean women with whom I became friendly was a Jehovah's Witness. Mrs. Im visited me nearly every Saturday. A pleasant woman, her original mission had been to convert me, or at least to save my soul. But eventually, she came simply for tea and conversation, no doubt subconsciously aware that I was beyond the pale, although she always began our conversations with some biblical commentary. She was very intelligent, and we had marvelous conversations. Her English was excellent, better than that of most other Koreans I encountered who had not lived in the U.S. We spoke of many things during her visits, and we shared food—in the way woman relate to each other throughout the world. She brought me kim-chi, and other homemade Korean foods such as bulgogi (Mongolian beef) one of my favorite Korean dishes. I gave her American food like chili and a spicy noodle bake. I found that Koreans didn't like bland food, so any version of American food I offered was spiked with ko-chu-chang, a Korean red-pepper paste.

One day, Mrs. Im told me she couldn't come the following week because all that week she would be making winter kim-chi. She said she didn't really want to make winter kim-chi but felt obligated to do it. Making kim-chi is a traditional wifely duty, and it is as arduous as a week of cleaning, chopping, and canning a couple hundred pounds of vegetables would be to an American woman. Very few would do it in this day and age. It's possible to purchase kim-chi in Korea, but the dutiful wife makes her own.

She had such a wistful expression on her face as she talked about making kim-chi that my heart went out to her. I had a small sense of the bondage in which she still found herself, and for which her Christianity brought some solace and hope. In fact, it was hope that she focused on whenever she talked with me about religion, and I could see it was hope that helped sustain her. My friendship with her gave me some insight into why Christianity has become so popular in Korea—and even why it might have spread so widely throughout the Roman Empire two millennia ago.

Another Korean woman I came to know in Songtan that first year was my landlady, Mrs. Yi. She lived in a downstairs apartment in the building she owned with her son. I assumed she was a widow. She also worked in the post office on base and spoke reasonably good English. She was always pleasant and upbeat. Her son took care of any repairs or problems I had in the apartment and, although he spoke essentially no English, his mother would translate for him. He was an excellent landlord, so I was unprepared for later difficulties with my landlord in Taegu.

While I was living in their apartment building in Songtan, Mrs. Yi had her sixty-year feast, a special birthday for elderly Koreans of either gender, which signifies a milestone in their lives. Afterwards, they become especially honored elders and are not expected to work (except to wait on husbands if they're women). After her sixty-year feast, I saw very little of Mrs. Yi. I remember her saying with some wistfulness that she would not be able to work on base anymore. I tried assuring her she could work as long as she wanted to, but she just shook her head. Sixty seemed to be the mandatory retirement age in Korea.

The only other Korean women I came to know fairly well that first year were two who worked for UMUC—one in the office at Osan AFB and one at Yongsan in the main office at Seoul. The first, married to a retired American serviceman, was vivacious and outgoing. She shepherded me around Osan AFB to the offices and merchants I needed to deal with. She taught me the phrase, *pali, pali,* Korean for 'hurry, hurry,' as we rushed from one spot to another on errands. The other arranged for living quarters and dealt with other logistical issues. She figured out how to purchase biology lab supplies locally and generally helped make my stay in Taegu tolerable. Both were immensely useful in negotiating the labyrinth of local and military customs and rules. But I never had a chance to know them much beyond our practical interactions.

During the second year, living in Taegu, the local Korean liaison for UMUC was not so helpful. However, I had the very good fortune of making friends with Mrs. Kim, a wonderful woman in her mid-to-late thirties who was the proprietress of a furniture store half a block from my apartment. I believe that, without the solace of her friendship as well as her intermittent help with local city villagers (merchants and others who dwelt in the same little alley), it would have been an extremely trying year.

We first became acquainted when I bought a few items in her furniture store to send to friends and relatives as presents that fall and winter. She was warm and outgoing, and she invited me for tea as I wandered around the shop trying to decide on purchases. Soon, she was bringing me kim-chi every week, always afraid I would not have enough and offering more. And I would reciprocate by bringing lunch to her place once or twice a week because she couldn't leave the furniture shop. As we were eating or having tea, we each tried to learn as much as we could of the other's language using dictionaries and old textbooks, pointing, and pronouncing words. I won't say that our attempts were completely unsuccessful; we both probably learned more than we realized. But it was often frustrating for both of us, and we had many misunderstandings I was aware of and probably many more I didn't even realize.

Mrs. Kim's husband was rarely at the shop, although I did meet him occasionally. I pieced together some of the facets of her life in our halting efforts at communication. She was, I believe, the first wife, that is, the legal wife. But she had no children, and her husband may have had another family, including children, in the country where he often stayed. He was absent from Taegu for days at a time. That didn't dampen her natural good humor, but then she had sources of personal affirmation and pride, including the furniture store. Her husband helped primarily by buying and transporting wooden products from sources in the countryside. But it seemed to be her shop.

She also had a number of women friends who visited for tea and riotous conversation. I dropped into the store one afternoon while they were there, and Mrs. Kim made an attempt at introductions. She seemed almost embarrassed that they were having such a good time. Perhaps she felt concern for me because I was an older woman alone in that unfamiliar alley among strangers. I feel certain that I was somehow under her protection because after I came to know her I had very little trouble with mischief or hostility from neighbors, whereas I had experienced hostility previously, particularly from a grocery shopkeeper across the alley from my apartment.

The other neighbor I came to know was a young woman who lived upstairs. She had a baby about a year old, but I never saw a husband. She, too, occasionally brought me traditional food of the kim-chi and sticky rice cake variety. I sometimes gave her food, but more often I brought her small things for the baby from the BX. I became overloaded with kim-chi in the refrigerator, as I could eat only a small amount of it with any dinner and had to gently put a brake on its flow from my local sources.

This young mother, whose name I do not remember, was sweet but sad-looking, and I saw her often late at night after I returned from evening classes, pacing back and forth with the baby bundled on her back in a typical Korean baby sling, looking up and down the main street where the end of the alley joined it, as if waiting for something or someone. My sense was that she spent her life in waiting. Was she a second wife? An unwed mother? How did she survive? Get food? Pay her rent? I might have asked Mrs. Kim—I'm guessing she would have known. But I didn't know how to ask and probably would not have understood her answers.

Even sadder than the women waiting and alone were the women who were beaten, especially in public. This was a phenomenon that Americans I met in Korea found very disturbing. It's not that women aren't beaten in the U.S., but it's rarely done in public and is considered criminal, or at least pathological. In Korea it seemed culturally acceptable. On more than one occasion—at railroad stations for some reason—I saw a woman lying on a sidewalk while being beaten by a man who was shouting at her in Korean, she with an arm over her head trying to protect her face, he holding her by the other arm and dragging her, clothes in disarray. Other American colleagues and occasional G.I. students also commented on public beatings they observed, with no one in the crowd making any effort to intervene on the woman's behalf. Sometimes a crowd gathered; often people just walked around the scene as if it were simply someone else's business.

In both Songtan and Taegu, a neighbor woman was frequently beaten somewhere near my apartment. I could hear wailing and shouting and sometimes rough, reverberating thumps and crashes, usually at night as I was lying in bed. In Songtan, the cries and shouts came from one of the houses behind my apartment building, easily heard in summer through an open back balcony door. In Taegu, where the apartments were crammed closely together, I could hear occasional thumping blows as well as screams and shouting, but I couldn't tell where they came from.

The women who were abused for money, such as the "juicy girls" mentioned in an earlier chapter, were placed in white slavery establishments largely through the willingness of their families. This might be for monetary gain, or because the families didn't have the financial means for giving them a decent marriage, or because there were too many other children, or simply because a female might be valued more as a commodity than as a person—at least, until she marries and has a male child.

Given the apparently insatiable sexual appetites of men who control most of the power and financial resources throughout the globe, it is not surprising that women are objects of sexual exploitation, especially in Asia, where females are generally valued less as citizens than as servants. It is tempting to use the phrase "victims of sexual exploitation" even if some women are complicit in that activity. In one railroad station, I saw a mother of a girl, perhaps eight or nine years of age, place the child at the door of the men's restroom. When the child came running back to her, the mother scolded her and pushed her back there again. After that, the child stood, docile, in her place. There is only one purpose I can imagine for that mother to station that child at that doorway. Perhaps the mother was financially desperate. But once the girl had accepted that activity, the obedient child could accept many other abuses of her personhood.

Some of the acquiescence to sexual exploitation by Korean women may be a legacy of the Japanese occupation (1905 – '45). During that time about 100,000 Korean women were sent to Japanese military camps as "comfort women." This shared shame among Korean women—yet to be admitted or redressed by the Japanese—may have lessened the social stigma of sexual abuse, but it may also have decreased the horror and outrage at such abuse as it continues to exist.

There is a Korean legend, often repeated, concerning a very large and sonorous bell called the Emilie Bell. The legend relates that craftsmen for several monarchs of the Silla Kingdom (Kings Songdok, Kyongdok and Hyegong) had attempted to make a huge and "heavenly" metal bell, but had repeatedly failed. Whenever they tried to make one, the bell would develop a crack or the tone would be dull. Finally, they were told by an astrologer (no doubt a male shaman) that in order to make a perfect bell, an innocent child had to be sacrificed.

A monk at court remembered that he had sought alms from a poor woman who said she had nothing to offer but her baby girl. Several officials and the monk visited the woman and wrenched the child from her mother's arms while both mother and child cried out for each other—the wail *emilie*. The child was cast into the vat of molten brass, the mixture was cast into its mold, and a "perfect bell" was produced. The heavenly sound of this bell (which currently rests in the National Kyongju Museum) rings with an overtone of *e-mi-li-e*, the sound of the child calling out for her mother.

Since I first heard it, I have tried to digest the meaning of this legend—its insight into the traditional spiritual landscape of Korea and its impact on the psyche of girls and women. I cannot think of it without feeling a tightening of my chest and abdomen and a deep sense of grief that such a fable is so often and openly—even proudly—repeated.

Chapter 14

ENVIRONMENTALLY FRIENDLY KOREA

"This is definitely a survival culture," said one of my students, a linguist in military intelligence who was married to a Korean woman. Koreans use everything—over and over again. One of the most positive impressions I retained from my stay in Korea was the environmental friendliness of its culture and practices. Koreans are serious recyclers; most household trash is recycled: glass, metal, plastic, paper. As much as one might deplore the trash piles heaped here and there in cities and around the countryside, these indicate an intensely saving culture.

Piles of wood—from pallets, renovated buildings, trimmed tree branches—are dried and used for heating or chipped and plowed into fields. In general, anything organic is recycled as fertilizer, including animal and even human wastes. This means that Koreans need little commercial fertilizer for their fields. Also, a water fern (*Azolla*) co-exists with an autotrophic bacterium (*Anabena*) in the flooded rice fields, a combination of organisms producing nitrogen-containing nutrients for the soil, so the rice fields are organically self regenerating.

Koreans rotate crops and grow two and sometimes three crops on a given piece of land in a year. In the winter, crops are grown mostly in long, plastic-covered, metal-ribbed, Quonset-style greenhouses that cover the fields. The vast amount of plastic used to cover these greenhouses is carefully folded and reused year after year.

Virtually every square foot of low-lying countryside is cultivated in small plots, perhaps an acre or two in size, using miniature, all-purpose tractors that can plow, till, plant, and pump water from the elaborate system of irrigation channels associated with every river and stream that flows out of the mountains. These mountains give Koreans a fairly reliable water supply. Fields are flooded with water from the spring run-off prior to planting rice shoots, a major determinant of the agricultural cycle.

Every piece of empty land that is not too steeply inclined and not too rocky is used for cultivation of spring, summer and fall crops. Even in cities and towns, squash vines cling to door-frames, and corn grows in rows below high-rise apartment buildings. The ubiquitous red peppers festoon narrow plots beside homes and along streets in both city and countryside. A lawn of grass yielding nothing edible would be unthinkable.

Human living quarters are generally constructed in an environmentally friendly way. In the countryside, family compounds cluster in villages between the fields and mountains. In cities, dwellings are mostly high-rise buildings at the perimeter of the main downtown area rather than single-family suburban homes sprawled across the countryside as in the U.S. Thus, human living space rarely encroaches upon crop land in the valleys and does not desecrate the tree-lined hills above. In fact, there is little construction in the mountains except for an occasional Buddhist temple. A few small sections of mountainside trees are cut here and there for timber, but these seem to be immediately replanted.

The existence of abundant forests in the hills and mountains of much of South Korea today is a recent phenomenon. Within the memory of many, including American veterans of the Korean

War with whom I have spoken, the hills and mountains were mostly denuded of trees. This was a consequence of deforestation by the Japanese as well as of scavenging by Koreans for building and heating during and after the horrors of the Korean War. A national effort at reforestation was promoted during the 1960s and '70s under Korea's President Park Chung-hee, father of the current president. With new growth of trees, carbon-dioxide clearing and oxygen-regenerating capacity have been restored to the hills and mountainsides, as has water-retention of the soil. Of course, there are small, cleared swatches in the mountains for the ubiquitous grave mounds, but these take up very little area, much less than one percent of the total forested mountainsides.

Amazingly, nobody takes what someone else has planted or harvested. In that regard, Koreans are extremely honest: they will not take what belongs to someone else if it is lying along the street. They are wily merchants and might overcharge you in the market, but they will not take your belongings. On the other hand, they are very willing to use what others have thrown away. A perfectly good umbrella, left in the hallway of our apartment building by someone who had moved out, remained there for several days until a colleague placed it in a trash can, whereupon it soon disappeared.

One of the early Korean industrialists apparently made his initial fortune by collecting and reusing or selling the trash from U.S. military bases. When I drove to the education center at Osan AFB in my Hyundai, I often saw Koreans nosing about the four large trash bins by the back parking lot. Such activity is certainly no shame; indeed, access to trash of the American military is considered a lucky opportunity. Once, on a bus ride from Kimpo (Seoul Airport) back to Songtan after a trip to Thailand, a Korean man began talking with me when he discovered I taught at the airbase. He bemoaned the fact that his trash pick-up contract at Osan AFB had been lost to a competitor. He thought perhaps I might be able to put in a good word for him with the powers that be. I assured him I had no idea how such things were decided and had no influence with the American military.

Koreans make good use of public transportation, which saves fuel resources in a country that possesses few energy resources of its own. Buses run on a fairly regular schedule with variable numbers of passengers, and trains run regularly and are usually packed. Unfortunately, Koreans have picked up one bad habit from Westerners—the love of cars.

The Korean male's auto devotion, verging on obsession, rivals that of Americans of the '50s. Owners tend their cars lovingly, polish them daily, and buy new ones every two or three years. Taxi drivers have an envied profession because they can drive around all day and night while earning money. Many of them, if they have a good driving record, own their own vehicles, although they may work for a cab company.

Koreans feel compelled to take their cars out for long drives on weekends, and they visit relatives in the country on every Korean holiday, of which there are many. Then, on the crowded roads, the cars creep along slowly in clots of traffic and apparently waste billions of *won* on fuel. Americans with UMUC were warned not to travel on the highways during major Korean holidays, and if we were required to go somewhere—to teach a class for example—we had to purchase our bus or train tickets early. I was told that taxis, as well as some cars, burn propane, which is cheaper than gasoline but much more dangerous in a collision because propane is more volatile and flammable than regular gasoline.

Perhaps for reasons of status, Koreans don't like to drive old cars, so transient Americans often inherit the junkers and clunkers, which base mechanics or Korean locals can usually transform into functional vehicles. Even if not in optimal running order, these vehicles perform sufficiently well to pass inspection and then are

Korea, Are You at Peace?

sold for little or nothing to another transient who rotates through. This was the type of car I drove while in Korea: first a 1988 Hyundai and then a 1990 Daewoo Espero. Despite their age, they were well-made vehicles and took me reliably throughout the countryside those two years in Korea.

Gardens between apartment buildings in Songtan

Chapter 15

LASTING IMPRESSIONS, LAND OF MORNING CALM

Recalling the scenes and experiences of two years in Korea, what images appear in my mind's eye? What new sights, sounds and tastes have been added to my sensory repertoire to transform the way I see the world? Kim-chi pots decorating patios and apartment rooftops. Tangy food spiced with hot pepper, garlic, and herbs. Dancing women in long, colorful, high-waisted silk dresses accompanied by whining strings and staccato drums.

Recollections of the Korean countryside were of picturesque and serene landscapes. A quilt work of rice fields in valleys. Sun rising in mist hovering over mountains. Rocks jutting from high, craggy, slopes. Buddhist temples with brilliantly colored flying eaves above peaceful courtyards. Clusters of half-melon grave mounds along mountainsides. Villages with brightly tiled roofs jutting above walled enclosures. Red peppers drying on mats alongside village roads.

In contrast to the singular charm and modest beauty of the Korean countryside, cities were generally unappealing. Shouts of men and growling of traffic in the general din and chaos of city streets. Cracking cement covered with dust and spittle in bus and train stations. Dark and uninviting flop-houses (yogwans). Sleazy karaoke bars in dark city alleys, and even sleazier bars around military bases.

Korea, Are You at Peace?

The most disagreeable aspect of my experience in Korea was the shabbiness of public spaces—dust everywhere and little greenery; chipping paint and ceramic on walls; cracked and eroding cement on floors and walkways. Unfortunately, this is what most visitors see initially in places of public transportation, along city streets and on the facades of city buildings whether public or private. And because Koreans don't waste anything, mounds of trash crop up in lots where nothing edible is growing. The trash grows and rusts with time. Presumably, trash pickers take what they want of it, and what remains becomes a permanent eye-sore. Such trash piles can be found every couple of city blocks, sometimes near what is clearly an active business establishment. This rusting trash reminded me of roadside scenes in American Appalachia, but the trash in Korean cities was in the middle of cement-covered, crowded areas, where no vegetation will eventually grow to shroud the decaying metal skeletons of useless things.

The most charming and picturesque places in cities, such as family courtyards, memorials and temple grounds, were usually hidden behind walls. Koreans take good care of interior spaces—their houses, cars, courtyards, and other places they own, including field plots. But public places—such as streets, bus stations, and other communal areas—are left to accumulate dust, dirt, decay, rot, and spittle.

Many historical and cultural reasons underlie the shabbiness that permeates heavily populated areas. Korean cities, the roads within them, and the highways connecting them have grown and spread for the most part during the past fifty years—since the end of the Korean War—and to a considerable extent under American influence. I was told that the American military largely paid for construction of the main throughway that connects Pusan to Seoul, the Kyongbu (Gyeongbu) Expressway, for logistical reasons. Because everything was built quickly, perhaps by those with little experience, mistakes were made and shoddy workmanship and inferior materials were sometimes used. The current degradation is a logical consequence of the process. The American military is not a sound model to follow for creating infrastructure. Military mentality focuses on the short term and, of necessity, tolerates a fair amount of ineptitude. It also has its share of graft and corruption where contractors are concerned, as do all political (and many civilian) entities.

But during the first half of the twentieth century, even before the Korean War, the Japanese annexed Korea and effectively pillaged the land and its people. They transported hundreds of thousands, mostly men, out of the country, either to farm in Manchuria or to work the mines in Japan. Thousands of Korean women were sent to Japanese military camps as comfort women. The Japanese closed most Korean schools and forbade Korean language publications. Korea became part of Japan but Koreans had no citizenship. The large Korean remnant living in Japan still does not have citizenship there.

Following World War II, Korea was arbitrarily divided between the superpowers, perhaps less brutal than the Japanese but still intending to control the politics and economy of the country. In the ensuing Korean War, which was really between the superpowers of East and West with their many pretexts for intervention, Korea once again became a battleground. The countryside was devastated during four great military sweeps as the battle raged down and up the peninsula. The initial invasion came from North Korea and drove south, overrunning Seoul and about two-thirds of South Korean territory. The invaders were pushed back north again, to the borders of (and briefly into) China. Then, with the help of China this time, the front moved south again, nearly to the Pusan perimeter and was once again repulsed northward just beyond the 38th parallel. The misery wrought on the country and its people was as dreadful as the devastation of any other modern war. It may have been more destructive than the Japanese occupation of the previous half century. In the process, those Koreans who survived learned how to make do with what scraps of food and debris they could find to sustain themselves.

While I was in Taegu, the streets—and those few sidewalks that existed—were frequently dug up because of the constant need for repairs of public structures such as water and sewage mains. Piles of sand, bricks, and cement slabs littered the edges of work areas. Of course, the same could be said for American cities. Cities tend to decay and become unlivable; they must be constantly rebuilt or else abandoned. But Korean cities don't seem to have well-maintained, user-friendly hubs of public transportation that are readily accessible to tourists.

Embedded in the bustle and chaos of Seoul are two remnants of a past era: Kyongbok Palace and Tosku Palace. Both survived the Japanese occupation and the Korean War and are islands of beauty and serenity, even though noises of honking and jack-hammers breach the walls from the streets outside, and construction cranes and high-rise buildings angle above them. These ancient oases provide some idea of what it might have been like, once upon a time, in Choson, Land of Morning Calm. However, this serenity and beauty were not accessible to the vast majority of Koreans of previous centuries.

Isabella Bishop received several invitations to attend the palace during her stays in Seoul, and was even allowed to photograph palace buildings, some of which she included in *Korea and Her Neighbors*. The palace grounds contrasted sharply with the crowded squalor she found outside its walls. Now, the palaces of Seoul are among the most pleasant tourist sites in the city.

Outside of shabby cities and towns extends the peaceful countryside, my most fondly remembered aspect of Korea. Much of the country is mountainous, and the mountains are old and subdued.

J. A. V. Simson

Korean mountains are largely covered by trees, with crumbling rock faces jutting from steeper slopes. Although once mostly denuded of trees, the mountains now project a lush and serene spectacle. The same happened in the Appalachians during the pioneer era of American history. In both cases, the trees have largely grown back, a result of government regulation and population redistribution.

I also felt a particular affinity for Koreans in their fondness for rocks. I, too, am a rock lover, and find character and beauty in the distorted irregularity of natural boulders and stones as well as in the design and symmetry of worked minerals. Koreans use rocks as decorations, carve inscriptions on them as memorials, and use them to construct walls and to shore up terraces. Rocks are everywhere in the mountains. Rocks, like trees, remind Koreans of the countryside and of their cultural roots. A decorative terrace in front of a building will consist mostly of rocks chosen for esthetic appeal, with bits of greenery growing in and among them. Grave mounds dotting the mountains also became, for me, an iconic image of Korea.

A charming feature of the Korean countryside is the farming village, usually consisting of ten to thirty buildings on a fairly level area along the lower slope of a mountain, with a dirt road winding up to it from the fields. The whole village is usually surrounded by several-feet-high walls enclosing family compounds. The compounds consist of two to four buildings surrounding a courtyard that may also be walled off from the rest of the village. Most of what one sees from the highway is the colorful mosaic of gently sloping tiled roofs—blue, red, green, and sometimes gray—atop the main buildings of each compound. This charming Korean village nestled low in the mountains is, I believe, a major cultural signature of the nation, and it informs the everyday mindset of many—perhaps most—Koreans.

In the valley below each village is a patchwork of fields, mostly rice fields, which stretch between mountains and are terraced into the lower hills, a sight I came to love and now miss since returning to the U.S. Virtually every available square foot of tillable land is cultivated, even in cities. What is not cemented over, as in cities, or rising steeply, as in mountains, has something growing upon it, planted and tended by local residents.

In the countryside, this would be a man with a tractor doing the big jobs—plowing, pumping water to flood the fields, harvesting. And nearby would be a woman with a straw hat covered by a kerchief pulled tight under her chin, bent over or squatting in the fields—planting, thinning, weeding. They might ride from the village to the fields and back together on the tractor—he driving, she standing on a strut over the rear wheels. One of my recurring pleasures, as I rode from place to place, was to look out a bus or train window and see these Korean couples working in the fields, although for them it must have been grueling.

The industry of Koreans in food production and food distribution is prodigious. Fields and the irrigation systems are ordered and well tended in the countryside, unlike public areas in the cities. A full century before my visit, Isabella Bishop foresaw that Koreans, if they were ever freed from the oppressive domination of the yangban, would be an industrious and productive people. South Korea's productivity has borne out her prediction. North Korea's people are still in bondage—to a different system of oppression.

A frustrating aspect of being a visitor in Korea is that most Koreans do not speak English, the *lingua franca* of our time, or any language besides Korean as far as I could tell, except in sleazy towns that surround American military bases. Older Koreans often speak Japanese because their schooling was in Japanese before the end of World War II. Although younger Koreans study English in school for several years, Korean and English are so dissimilar, and most Koreans have so little use for English, that it evaporates from their memories shortly after they leave school unless they work in a tourist agency or on an American military base. The same can be said of Americans of course. Even if they have studied a language in school, most can't use it after they graduate.

Even in tourist spots in Korea, it was difficult for me to find anyone who spoke English. I visited Building 63, a high-rise building towering over the cityscape of Seoul and a major tourist spot containing restaurants and an aquarium. But I could find no one who spoke English at a desk beneath an INFORMATION sign displayed prominently in English. Some Korean friends had said they would meet me at the information desk, and it took me nearly half an hour to find someone who spoke English, a manager from another part of the building. As it happened, there were two information desks in the building. I did meet my friends, well after our arranged time. If English were spoken more commonly, it would open up tourism to Europeans and Americans. Perhaps the Hermit Kingdom mentality, which prevailed when Isabella Bishop was there, persists in some recess of the collective Korean psyche.

As I came to know Koreans, it became clear that there were as many different personality types as exist in any other culture. Listening to the tone and temper of conversations on the street though, I had the impression that men tended to be emphatic to the point of dogmatism and women tended to be argumentative or whiny. Children seemed to cry a lot—perhaps because they usually got their way when they cried. Koreans care very much for their children, in the family and in the culture as a whole. Children may walk unattended along busy city streets, and, although Koreans often drive like madmen, if a child wants to cross a street, he simply raises an arm in the air, and cars will stop to let him cross.

The Korean temperament seems to reflect the love for red pepper—spicy and energetic, perhaps more than other East Asian nationalities. My take-away impression: Koreans were private and opinionated individuals who were quick to judge and quick to forgive, who were willing to work, who liked to eat and drink well, and who became more appealing the better I came to know them.

Of all the places I visited in Korea, Kyongju was my favorite town. It was the capital of the ancient Silla Kingdom and was rich in cultural artifacts—truly a living museum. Because it lay southeast of the Pusan Perimeter, it was spared the ravages of bombardment and looting that occurred throughout the rest of the country during the Korean War. It is a beautiful site on a plain, surrounded by high, rolling hills and low mountains. The plain itself undulates with man-made mounds that serve as repositories for the remains of Silla royalty from the first millennium C.E. The museum there contains a wonderful collection of ancient artifacts spanning Korean history from the Neolithic period into the Yi dynasty. I was sorry I could not visit Kyongju a third time before my departure.

Although tourists may experience superficial public shabbiness and difficulties with communication, Korea repays a visit multifold and offers rewards found in no other country. If a visitor is willing to go into the countryside, view the villages and the mountains, and interact with people, something ineffable can happen. Awe at the utter charm of Korean country villages. A sense of peace in the mountains in the morning. Amazement at the exuberant colors of Buddhist temples. Admiration for the self-sufficiency and industry of Korean people. Surprise at the beauty and endurance of so many artifacts of the ancient Silla Kingdom.

Isabella Bishop left Korea in 1897, *"with Russia and Japan facing each other across their destinies."*[52] She claimed that her early distaste for Korea had mellowed into kindliness, almost affection, and that she was truly sorry to leave the country.

I left Korea with an impression of Korea as the Asian version of Switzerland (where I had previously spent a sabbatical year). It is a mountainous country, dotted with quaint farming villages in which live sturdy, self-sufficient, independent individuals, who don't want

J. A. V. Simson

to have too much to do with the rest of the world. Yet South Korea, at least, is a country with real heart—almost naiveté—separated from other, more militant and callous nations by thin strips of sea, and from its dangerous (yet longed-for) brother nation, North Korea, by a very narrow strip of land, the DMZ.

Gentle mountains in south-eastern Korea

Appendix

AN OVERVIEW OF KOREAN HISTORY

Korean history prior to the major Korean War of the mid-twentieth century receives essentially no coverage in Western textbooks. This may be partly because no story of romance or intrigue hovers over this land. Throughout its history, Korea has preferred to remain a Hermit Kingdom *vis-à-vis* its neighbors and the world, limiting its contact with outside cultures except Chinese. Several East Asian countries have entered the textbooks because adventurers and popularizers have visited them. But Korea has had no such cultural champions.

We learn something of the history of China, a major world power for millennia, motivated initially by Marco Polo's travels and later by the novels of Pearl S. Buck. We are exposed to Japanese history and art, once it was opened to the West by an American, Admiral Perry, and popularized by Italian and British musicians—Puccini and Gilbert and Sullivan. After its World War II defeat in 1945, Japan was rehabilitated financially by the American Marshall Plan and culturally by the industry and financial acumen of its population. We learn about India from extensive British contacts and the novels and stories of E.M. Forster and Rudyard Kipling. We develop an interest in Thailand (Siam) from books and movies derived from the 1944 novel *Anna and the King of Siam*.

But Korea has had no popularizer and consequently no

demanding fans to draw the attention of Western academics and artists to its culture and history. Moreover, much of the country's historic legacy—and a great many cultural artifacts illuminating that history—were destroyed during the first half of the twentieth century. This came about by a combination of the Japanese occupation from 1905 to the end of World War II followed by the Korean War between the northern and southern halves of the country, promulgated largely by cold war fears and the ambitions of the world powers: USSR, U.S., and China. The following thumbnail sketch of the cultural and political history of Korea is offered as a supplement to the chapters in this volume.[53]

The Korean peninsula was probably settled in several waves during the great eastward migration of *Homo sapiens* prior to the end of the last ice age—a movement that also populated the Americas. The settlers came from the high Asian plateau and northern China, the area of origin of many restless and wandering tribes that swept both eastward and westward in prehistoric and historic times. Several factors—genetic and cultural analyses of Korean people, the Korean language, and ancient Korean artifacts—all point to their origin as Tungus peoples from northeast Asia, related to Mongols, who have periodically descended from the high Asian plateau to conquer and then assimilate into surrounding cultures. Several migrations probably penetrated into the peninsula in Korea's pre-dynastic period (prior to 500 B.C.E.), but the culture retained its basically animistic roots well into the first millennium of the Common Era. The early wanderers were stone-age hunters and gatherers who, on populating the Korean *cul-de-sac*, apparently found its abundant fish and mountain forests a congenial environment that quelled their restless spirit.

Korea had its Bronze Age, beginning about 1000 B.C.E. and an Iron Age about five centuries later. The use of forged metals in Korea—as elsewhere in Asia and Europe—led to a warrior culture and the establishment of kingdoms. About two centuries before the Common Era, three kingdoms occupied most of the Korean peninsula: Koguryo (Goguryeo), Silla (Shilla) and Paekche (Baekje). These kingdoms included varying but substantial regions of what is now Manchuria. Indeed, the Koreans' most sacred mountain, Mt. Paektu, is located on the border of North Korea and China. This is a volcanic mountain, considered by many Koreans their ancestral home, with a "heavenly lake" filling its caldera.

The Three Kingdoms were enlargements and consolidations of what were initially city states and their environs. The Three Kingdoms period spanned about eight centuries between the end of the second century B.C.E. to the end of the seventh century C.E., when much of the this territory was unified under the Silla Kingdom.

The northern state was Koguryo, the most extensive of the Three Kingdoms. This kingdom engaged in frequent conflicts with China at their common borders. Several centuries later, Koguryo was replaced by Koryo, from which came the name Korea, as used in Western countries. In the southern part of the peninsula were Paekje and Silla. These two kingdoms were ruled dynastically on the Chinese model, with occasional changes in dynasty resulting from a military coup or conquest by a neighbor.

In a series of battles lasting half a century, the Silla Kingdom consolidated power over much of the Korean peninsula, incorporating Paekje and much of Koguryo under its domain. It became known as the Unified Silla Kingdom with its capital at Kyongju. Silla maintained its dominance until replaced in the tenth century by the kingdom of Koryo, the expanded and revitalized rump state of Koguryo.

The Silla Kingdom was significant for many reasons. It had what many consider the longest ruling dynasty in world history, lasting from 109 B.C.E until 935 C.E., more than a thousand years. This was also a period of high cultural development in Korea, when the country produced its own style of building, arts, and ceramics, as well as its practical and social customs relating to food production and the family. Koreans borrowed and greatly simplified Chinese styles of pottery, dress, and decor. This modified Chinese culture was then passed on to the Japanese in an eastward flow of artifacts, religion, and civilized behavior. Cultural artifacts from the Silla Kingdom period are more plentiful than those from most of the rest of Korean history because the center of the kingdom lay in the southeastern part of the peninsula, and this region was protected during the Korean War of the mid-twentieth century. The Unified Silla Kingdom endured until the early tenth century C.E., when it was overthrown by General Wang Kon, who founded the Koryo Kingdom.

The Koryo Kingdom lasted from the tenth until the late fourteenth century, and became a highly hierarchical society, with slavery and other forms of servitude being the hereditary lot of the lower classes. It was during this period that both Buddhism and Confucianism became deeply rooted in the political and cultural life of Korea, accompanied by the building of Buddhist temples and the establishment of Confucian academies. Court culture, especially music and dance, was heavily influenced by close cultural ties with China during that country's Tang and Sung dynasties.

Whatever cultural influences they received from their powerful neighbor was layered upon a vigorous native music and dance heritage, largely shamanistic in origin. It was also during this period that the exquisite pale green celadon ceramic was developed, the signature Korean pottery recently revived by contemporary artisans. An important cultural innovation in the early thirteenth century was movable block printing, first developed in Korea, with a Chinese ideograph on each block. This preceded movable type in the West by more than a century.

Around this time, the Koryo Kingdom was harassed by Mongol invaders, as was its larger neighbor and protector, China, which eventually succumbed. Korea ultimately paid homage (and tribute) to the Yuan dynasty, the Mongol dynasty in power when Marco Polo visited China in the late thirteenth century. Wars with the Mongols and other northern invaders, coupled with Japanese piracy off the eastern coast, ultimately weakened the political structure.

The Koryo Kingdom was overthrown by General Yi Song-gye, who established the Yi Dynasty in the late fourteenth century. The Yi Dynasty, ruling what is often referred to as the Kingdom of Choson (currently transliterated Joseon), survived until the Japanese occupation of Korea in the early twentieth century. Isabella Bishop arrived in Korea during the late Yi Dynasty, which was overthrown by Japan shortly after her departure.

The early Yi Dynasty (Choson) was a period of considerable stability and cultural development. It established a rigid, hereditary social hierarchy consisting of four classes: yangban, chungin, sangmin, and ch'onmin. Education—and thus political control—was limited to the yangban class in Korea, This strict hierarchy contrasted with the Chinese system, in which educated commoners could rise to high status. However, the Korean class system may have been less oppressive than in other countries because it was not necessarily related to wealth. Most Koreans of the period, including yangban, were farmers, and education had a higher cultural value than did wealth. Moreover, strong family ties, a key precept of Confucianism, sustained family support systems within all classes. Perhaps because of the strong Buddhist influence, Koreans did not have a cultural tradition of ostentation, so taxation for the sake of pomp—typically exhibited by aristocrats in many cultures—might not have afflicted the Korean lower classes as much as peoples living under other hierarchical political systems.

It was during the Choson period that the unique Korean alphabet, Hangul, was developed and promulgated by King Sejong the Great, with the help of a group of linguists he had assembled at court. This is the simplest of the Eastern Asiatic scripts to learn and read because it is a phonetic alphabet, with words constructed in syllables. Thus, literacy was greater in Korea than in other Asian nations. Even court women learned to read. In fact, for a century or so after it was devised, Hangul was considered a women's script. Easy to read and write, it was also used by merchants, but the merchant class was held in some contempt by upper class Koreans. Thus, Hangul was not adopted by the yangban literati and did not come into wide usage in Korea until after the Japanese occupation. The script, as well as the Korean language itself, had been banned under the Japanese; hence it became a patriotic act to establish Hangul as the national script.

As with its predecessor, the Koryo Kingdom, Choson was harassed from the north by Manchu invaders and from the east by Japanese. In one major set of battles, Japanese invaders were eventually repulsed by a convoy of the famous armored "turtle ships" designed by Admiral Yi Sun-sin, a Korean hero. These were probably the first metal-covered ships in world history, and with their protective metal shells, they resisted damage by incendiary weaponry. With them, Admiral Yi inflicted a serious defeat upon Japanese pirates and military vessels.

The opening of Korea to the West was a painful and difficult process for the country as it was for other non-European countries. Korea managed to maintain its (pen)insularity for longer than most Asian countries, partly because of its distance from the major sailing routes of Spanish, Portuguese and English adventurers and traders, and partly because it had little to contribute to the spice or silk trades. This isolation no doubt reinforced the Hermit-Kingdom tradition.

Nonetheless, missionaries came, as they came to all lands around the globe, and brought with them Christianity and Western cultural assumptions, often at odds with local traditional values.

Catholicism was first introduced by Korean scholars from China, but it was initially ignored and then opposed by the government. At first, Christianity—called by Koreans Sohak or Western Learning—became something of a vogue among Korean scholars, many of whom became Catholics. Conversions happened partly because the Church brought with it reforms in education and health care for people without regard to class status, a practice that attracted many in the lower classes. By the mid-nineteenth century however, the upper class began to mount serious opposition to Christianity, mistrusting its egalitarianism as a potential threat of revolt. This opposition became state persecution, and several Catholic priests were executed.

Following the Catholics into Korea, groups of Methodist and Presbyterian missionaries came in the latter half of the nineteenth century. They also established schools and hospitals on the peninsula. It was largely through Protestant missionary connections that Isabella Bishop managed her travels around the Korean peninsula. At present, about half of Korean nationals who profess a religious faith claim to be Christian.

Resistance to Christianity and Westernization came not just from the government but also from an anti-government movement of the late eighteen-hundreds called *Tonghak* (Eastern Learning). This movement had a religious character and arose in reaction to Sohak (Western Learning), which was equated with Christianity. Near the end of the nineteenth century, the movement ultimately became the Tonghak rebellion. Its leaders demanded those economic and social reforms unjustly feared by the Korean monarchy. The complex history of Korea at the end of the nineteenth century cannot be properly understood without some consideration of this movement. It had a decidedly democratic ideology, but because of that, it alarmed Korean nobility, most particularly the king and his court.

Isabella Bishop described Tonghaks as largely idealistic reformers, and expressed sympathy for their condemnation of the rapacity and social unconcern of Korean officialdom.

> "The Tong-hak proclamation began by declaring in respectful language loyal allegiance to the king, and went on to state the grievances in very moderate terms. The Tong-haks asserted, and with undoubted truth, that officials in Korea, for their own purposes, closed the eyes and the ears of the King to all news and reports of the wrongs inflicted on his people...
> The necessity for reform was strongly urged. There were no expressions of hostility to foreigners, and the manifesto did not appear to take any account of them... For in the midst of the thousand wild rumors which were afloat, it appeared certain that the King sent several hundred soldiers against the Tong-haks... The King was supposed to be prepared for flight.
> ... [I]t is only with the object of showing with what an excellent pretext for interference the Tong-haks had furnished the Japanese that I recall this petty chapter of what is now ancient history."[54]

Concessions were made to the rebels in order to re-establish peace, but the Korean government appealed to China, as it often did when trouble was imminent. As it happened, this was a time of great political weakness on the part of the Chinese government, but China did send troops to Korea at the request of King Kojong. These troops were roundly defeated by Japanese troops, also in Korea at the time, ostensibly to protect Japanese shipping and trading interests.

It was also a period of complex court intrigue in Korea, with a weak king, King Kojong, dominated by the regent (*Taewongun*), who was an enemy of the king's wife, Queen Min. The Japanese, in the wings, were keenly aware of the weaknesses of both Chinese and Korean governments. In the First Sino-Japanese War (1894, '95), which took place on Korean soil, China was defeated, and Japanese power on the peninsula was solidified.

After a year-long trip to China (not chronicled in *Korea and Her Neighbors*), Isabella Bishop returned to Seoul and found the political situation very precarious. The king was, in effect, under the protection of the Russian legation, but he exerted his monarchical privileges with little wisdom. She described some success in efforts to clean up of the city of Seoul. Streets were widened and most garbage was removed. She also noted increased access to information via Korean language newspapers as well as reform of the prison system. But she despaired of Korean law, which had not been codified and could change at any time on the whim of the king.

Although Isabella Bishop saw much to concern her in the history and culture of Korea—especially in the laziness and rapacity of the upper class—she ended her travel narrative on an optimistic note, indicating that Korea had abundant resources and a good climate. She viewed the Western influence in Korea as salutary, and even remarked positively on the *"energetic ascendancy of Japan"*.[55] She seemed to view Japan's defeat of China as a positive result in separating Korea from the influence of a decadent neighbor. She was apparently self-deceived in writing, *"I believe that Japan was thoroughly honest in her efforts. . ."*[56] But she also did not believe that Japan had given up its interest in controlling at least some aspects of the Korean state. She observed: *"Japan for several centuries has regarded herself as possessing vested rights to commercial ascendancy in Korea."*[57]

Having developed plans for their own military hegemony over eastern Asia, the Japanese then decided to strike, using preservation of Korean autonomy as a pretext. This was done by means of a complex strategy combining diplomacy and military intervention in which Russia, China, Great Britain, France and the United States were complicit—foreshadowing later events in Korean politics of the twentieth century. During the debacle, Queen Min, the wife of King Kojong, was murdered in a conspiracy involving the Taewongun and supported by Japanese troops. The complexity of this situation has been exquisitely rendered in a recent Korean opera, *The Last Empress*.[58]

However, with the murder of Queen Min, the Japanese suffered a blow to their international prestige, and Russia gained influence in Korea. Nonetheless, Isabella Bishop noted the tenacity and fixity of purpose of the Japanese. Perhaps she was more in touch with the true Japanese intent in Korea than I thought on first reading the last chapter of her book, when she wrote,

> "To deprive China of a suzerainty which, it must be admitted, was not exercised for the advantage of Korea; to consolidate her (Japan's) own commercial supremacy; to ensure for herself free access and special privileges; to establish a virtual protectorate under which no foreign dictation would be tolerated; **to reform Korea on Japanese lines, and to substitute her own liberal and enlightened civilization for the antique oriental conservatism of the Peninsula**, are aims which have been kept steadily in view for forty years, replacing in part the designs which had existed for several previous centuries."[59] (my highlighting)

This assessment indicates, I think, that Isabella Bishop was indeed favorable to Japanese influence in Korea, despite its pernicious character. Perhaps she viewed the budding Japanese imperialist activity as a mirror of British imperialism, with its superior-civilization-and-culture assumptions and rhetoric.

Russia developed considerable influence on the peninsula at that time and even recommended the possible division of influence with Japan along a boundary near the 38th parallel. But the Russian monarchy was also weak, and it was soon to be overthrown by the Communist revolution during World War I. One factor contributing to the Czar's ouster was probably the Russian military defeat by Japan in Manchuria, leading to a treaty in 1905, signed by both the U.S. and Great Britain, in which Korea became a "protectorate" of Japan. The Japanese strategy in Korea was to use and then marginalize its weak ruler, a strategy they followed subsequently in China in the 1930s.

Thus in 1905, Korea was dominated by Japan and was officially annexed in 1910, leading to forty years of occupation and oppression that many Koreans view as the darkest period of their history. Although resistance and independence movements developed in Korea after the Japanese annexation, they were brutally suppressed.[60] Indeed, eventually even Korean language instruction was abolished on the peninsula, and Japanese became the "national language" of Korea from the mid-1930s until the end of World War II. However, anti-Japanese resistance was sustained by Koreans in exile, particularly in China.

As World War II drew to a close, the USSR declared war on Japan and began sending troops into the Korean peninsula from the north. Because the United States feared that Communist Russia would take over the entire country, the U.S. proposed dividing the country along the 38th parallel into two military operating zones, and Stalin accepted the proposal. After Japan's surrender, American troops landed in the south and put the southern half of the peninsula under U.S. military protection. Thus, the north became a Communist territory, heavily influenced by Russia, and the south remained under U.S. (and U.N.) military governance.

Particularly in the south, resentment against another occupying power grew strong. A provisional government was eventually formed in 1947 in South Korea with heavy American influence, and about that time Kim Il-Sung became the national dictator in North Korea with Soviet assistance. Democratic elections were finally held in the south in 1948. The elected officials established a Korean government with some legitimacy, called the Republic of Korea. However, both North and South Korean governments wanted the entire Korean peninsula to be part of their jurisdiction. Thus arose the two Koreas, a situation that continues to this day and is unsatisfactory to all parties involved.

Of course each Korea viewed the other half as occupied by hostile forces, so it was not surprising that war ensued. Most American troops were withdrawn from the south in 1949 and, in June of 1950, North Korea invaded the South with substantial Russian aid in the form of tanks and artillery. It was a *blitzkrieg*, and within days more than half of the Republic of Korea was overrun. American troops were quickly transferred back to Korea from Japan and, under the command of General MacArthur, maintained a position in the southeast of the country around Pusan, an important port and landing site for battleships.

This was the famous Pusan Perimeter, which MacArthur was determined to maintain at all costs. The United Nations rallied, and other nations began sending troops to aid South Korea. MacArthur's stunning landing at Inchon (a port town on the eastern side of the peninsula on the China Sea, not far from Seoul) isolated North Korean troops in the south, and as Communist troops withdrew northward, the battles were particularly fierce. South Korean and U.N. troops then invaded north, across the 38th parallel, and went as far as the Yalu River, the border between North Korea and China. At this point, the Chinese sent more than 100,000 troops with artillery into Korea. This contingent pushed the battle southward, and Seoul was again captured by northern forces. Once again, U.N. troops eventually forced the invaders back north across the

38th parallel. After three years of vicious fighting, in 1953 North Korea ultimately proposed a truce, brokered by the Soviets. This was an armistice, not a peace treaty. From a political perspective, the Korean War has never officially ended. War was never declared in the conflict, and no peace treaty was ever concluded among the battling parties.

After the end of active conflict on the peninsula (July 27, 1953), North Korea continued as a military dictatorship, initially under the protection of the USSR. Kim Il-sung, who was a hero in the struggle against the Japanese occupation, became the first leader of the DPRK, established in 1948. He was followed by his son, Kim Jong-il, in 1994. His grandson, Kim Jong-un has become the face of North Korea since 2011, although his actual status and power are not entirely clear. Since the fall of the Soviet Union, North Korea has been politically isolated, with China as its nominal protector.

A brief thaw between North and South occurred in 2000 – '01, during which time the "two Kims" (Kim Jong-il and Kim Dae-jung) – met briefly, but nothing substantial came of it. North Korea has become a rogue state, dropping out of the Nuclear Nonproliferation Treaty in 2003 and performing its first nuclear test that same year. There have been two further tests, the most recent in February of this year (2013) under Kim Jong-un. Although it is difficult to assess the social or financial situation of the country, it seems clear that the leadership's focus on military power has come at a cost of civilian well-being. A NASA view of the night sky showing darkness over North Korea bears this out.[61]

In the more than five decades since the truce, South Korea has gone through a series of political systems and political leaders, several of whom were military usurpers and more or less oppressive. However in the 1980s, democracy and economic reform began to take hold, and Korea has become one of the most prosperous nations in Asia— one of Asia's Four Little Tigers, referring to small, economically successful countries of East Asia. This period of Korean history has been ably and comprehensively chronicled in *The Two Koreas* by Don Oberdorfer.[62]

U.S. troops remain in South Korea. No doubt the U.S. did not want to make the mistake of another "hasty withdrawal" as occurred after WW II, particularly in light of the fact that the Koreas are still, technically, not at peace. U.S. military and support personnel constitute a substantial presence in Korea, although these are mostly sequestered in sites removed from main population centers. Of course, local populations are affected by the military presence, and local towns have grown up to service American military installations. It was under the auspices of the American military that UMUC was given a contract to teach college courses on military bases in Europe and Asia. And it was through UMUC that I had the privilege of teaching on military bases and traveling throughout the Republic of Korea. For this I am grateful.

Turtle ship replica, cherry blossoms, Chinhae

TRANSLITERATIONS OF KOREAN WORDS

Text place names and common words (2000 CE)	**Newer transliterations or alternative spellings**
Anjunri	Anjeong-ri
Chejudo	Jeju-do
Chinhae	Jinhae-gu
Choson	Joseon
Chungchongnam	Chungcheongnam
Inchon	Incheon
Kangnun	Gangneun
Kangwondo	Gangwon-do
Koguryo	Goguryeo
Kojong	Gojong
Kunsan	Gunsan
Kyongbu	Gyeongbu
Kyonggi-do	Gyeonggi-do
Kyongju	Gyeongju
Paekche	Baekje
Pyongt'aek,	Pyeongtaek
Pulguksa	Bulguksa
Pusan	Busan
Sokkuram	Seokguram
Sondok	Seondeok
Soraksan	Seoraksan
Taegu	Daegu
Tonghak	Donghak
yogwan	yeogwan

SUGGESTED READINGS

Bishop, Isabella Bird. *Korea and Her Neighbours*. 1897. Reprinted 1970. Yonsei University Press, Seoul, Korea.

Breen, Michael. *The Koreans: Who They Are, What They Want, Where Their Future Lies*. 1998, revised 2004.Thomas Dunne Books, St. Martin's Press, New York, NY.

Buck, Pearl S. *Living Reed, a Novel of Korea*. 1963. Beaufort Books, New York, NY.

Cumings, Bruce. *Korea's Place in the Sun: A Modern History*. 2005, revised edition. W.W. Norton & Company, New York, NY.

Covell, Jon Carter. *Korea's Cultural Roots*. 1982. Hollym International Corp., Elizabeth, NJ.

Fulton, Bruce and JuChan. *Wayfarer: New Fiction by Korean Women*. Edited and translated by B and J-C Fulton. 1997. Women in Translation, Seattle, WA.

Halberstam, David. *The Coldest Winter: America and the Korean War*. 2007. Hyperion, New York, NY.

Joe , Wanne J. *Traditional Korea, A Cultural History*. 1997. Hollym International Corp., Elizabeth, NJ.

Kaye, Evelyn. *Amazing Traveler: Isabella Bird*. 1937. Blue Penguin Publications, Boulder, CO, prepared by Quality Books Inc.

Mason, David A. *Spirit of the Mountains: Korea's SAN-SHIN and Traditions of Mountain Worship*. 1999. Hollym International Corp., Elizabeth, NJ.

Middleton, Dorothy. *Victorian Lady Travelers*. 1993 (second printing). Academy Chicago Publishers, Chicago, IL.

Murphey, Rhoads. *A History of Asia*, second Edition. 1996. HarperColiins College Publishers, New York, NY.

Nahm, Andrew C. *A Panorama of 5000 Years: Korean History*, second revised edition. 1989. Hollym International Corp., Elizabeth, NJ.

Nahm, Andrew C. *Introduction to Korean History and Culture*. 1994. Hollym International Corp., Elizabeth, NJ.

Oberdorfer, Don. *The Two Koreas: A Contemporary History*. 1997, revised 2001. Basic Books, New York, NY.

Robinson, Martin, Ray Bartlett and Rob Whyte. Korea. *Lonely Planet Guide*, 2007, Oakland, CA.

Saccone, Richard. *Travel Korea Your Way*. 1994. Hollym International Corp., Elizabeth, NJ.

Saccone, Richard. *Having a Great Tour. The G.I. Guide to Korea*. 1998. Hollym International Corp., Elizabeth, NJ.

Storey, Robert and David Mason. *Korea. Lonely Planet Guide.* 1997. Lonely Planet Publications, Hawthorn, Vie, Australia.

Winchester, Simon. *Korea. A Walk through the Land of Miracles*. 2005. Harper Perennial

Also:

Korean Heritage, Volume II. Korean Overseas Information Service. 1996. Hollym International Corp., Elizabeth, NJ.

ACKNOWLEDGEMENTS

As with all attempts at creativity, credit for a finished product must be shared with many others who have helped in the process and who have encouraged and tempered the author's own internal muses and demons. What follows cannot include all who have helped in ways of which they were not even aware, whose assistance lies submerged in my subconscious. I hope I have included all of my major assistants during the two years in Korea. And I wish particularly to thank those who have provided help and encouragement since my return to the United States, during the effort to coalesce the many Korean reminiscences into a travel narrative.

First, I wish to express my great appreciation to the University of Maryland, University College (UMUC), Overseas Division for the opportunity to teach and travel abroad (first in Asia and later in Europe). This extraordinary opportunity allowed a retired professor to see much more of the world than would otherwise have been possible. Most particularly, I would like to thank Rosemary Hoffmann for her graciousness upon our first meeting, and for subsequently offering me a job. In the Korean Office of UMUC Overseas (in Seoul), I would especially like to thank Irene Chung for her constant support and her good humor in the face of myriad complexities at the interface of university and military cultures. I also wish to extend deep appreciation to Jenny Ho for her tireless and efficient logistical support at the interface of university and local cultures during my two years in Korea. And I wish to thank

Mrs. Lee for her steady friendship during my second year in her country.

Since my return, several friends and relatives have assisted in the process of turning a jumble of disconnected journal entries, letters, photos, and e-mails into something resembling a travel story. The photographs illustrating this manuscript were taken during my two years in Korea. The map on the front piece is used by permission,[63] and that on the back flyleaf was hand-drawn by the author.

My daughter, Maria Simson, has been especially helpful with her editorial expertise. It was she who originally suggested that I interweave Isabella Bishop's experiences into my narrative, and she has helped enormously and repeatedly with editorial suggestions on several versions of the manuscript.

A long-time friend and fellow writer, Constance Pultz, (now deceased) read and commented on the original version, which required radical restructuring. Laura Moses performed excellent editorial corrections on a manuscript more or less midway in its evolution; these have been retained in the current version and have improved its overall quality. Three close friends, Skeet Godow, Marcia Brown, and Gayle Sauer read later versions completely through and offered suggestions and encouragement, although they were probably too kind in their evaluation of what was still a very rough manuscript. Carla Lowrey, another friend with writing and editorial experience, reviewed two versions of the manuscript and suggested changes and reorganizations that have contributed greatly to improving the narrative. Two long-time friends, Arthur Molella and Dinah Oakley, also read a recent version of the manuscript and made several useful suggestions. Additional editorial improvements have been made by Mary Johnston, Joanna Innes, Penny Travis, and Ellie and Ray Setser. In addition, I also extend gratitude to David Mason, a Korean scholar, who read the submission-ready manuscript and made several suggestions, most of which have been incorporated into the book. All those willing to read the manuscript in its various permutations have earned my deepest gratitude.

Any flaws or shortcomings in the present version of the book are my responsibility alone. I apologize in advance for any irreverence I may have shown in these pages toward persons, places, countries, cultural practices, ideologies, or even ideas. No offense was ever intended toward a country and a people for whom I have the greatest respect. I have simply presented what I saw, heard, read, and thought during my two years in Korea and in the subsequent incubation period of this book. My purpose is to provide a largely sympathetic picture of a country that doesn't sit for many portraits. I hope these efforts will serve to enlighten—and sometimes amuse—those who read it.

ENDNOTES

1. *Korea's Cultural Roots*. Jon Carter Covell. 1982. Hollym International Corp., Elizabeth, N.J.
2. *Korea and Her Neighbours*. Isabella Bird Bishop. 1897. Reprinted 1970. Yonsei University Press, Seoul, Korea
3. *Korea and Her Neighbours*. I.B. Bishop
4. *ibid.*, p. 26
5. *ibid.*, p. 13
6. *ibid.*, p. 38
7. *ibid.*, p. 124
8. *ibid.*, p. 40
9. *ibid.*, p. 101, 102
10. See the Appendix for more on the history of this tragic miscalculation. This is probably true of most wars.
11. Copyright 2013, Jo Anne Simson. Permission is granted to copy by Wikimedia Commons to distribute and/or modify this photograph under the terms of the "GNU Free Documentation License." Original by Kevin Rein.
12. *The Two Koreas: A Contemporary History*, by Don Oberdorfer, revised 2001, Basic Books
13. *The Coldest Winter: America and the Korean War*, by David Halberstam, 2007, Hyperion, NY
14. *Korea and Her Neighbours*. I.B. Bishop
15. *Korea's Cultural Roots*. Covel
16. *Korea and Her Neighbours*. I.B. Bishop, p. 71
17. *ibid.*, p. 84
18. *ibid.*, p. 88
19. *ibid.*, p. 86
20. *ibid.*, pp. 99, 100

21. *Spirit of the Mountains: Korea's SAN-SHIN and Traditions of Mountain Worship*. David A Mason. 1999. Hollym International Corp. Elizabeth, NJ
22. *ibid*, footnote 78, p124
23. *Korea and Her Neighbours*. I.B. Bishop, p. 118
24. *ibid.*, pp. 121, 122
25. *ibid.*, p. 125
26. *ibid.*, p. 134
27. *ibid.*, p. 137
28. *ibid.*, p. 193
29. *ibid.*, p. 196
30. This was Hill 180, site of a famous battle during the Korean War.
31. *ibid.*, p. 125.
32. *ibid.*, p. 137.
33. *ibid.*, p. 387
34. *ibid.* pp. 387, 388
35. See Fulton, Bruce and JuChan. *Wayfarer: New Fiction by Korean Women* for excellent translations of poignant Korean stories. referenced in Suggested Readings
36. I once happened upon a museum in Alaska, set up by a group of Native Americans who also called themselves the "Han People," but when I tried to talk with a museum attendant about the Han people in Asia, she didn't want to hear about it.
37. *Korea and Her Neighbours*. I.B. Bishop, p. 399
38. *Amazing Traveler: Isabella Bird*. Kaye, E., 1937. Blue Penguin Books
39. *Korea and Her Neighbours*. I.B. Bishop p. 426
40. *Korea's Cultural Roots*, by Jon Carter Covel, and *Traditional Korea, a Cultural History*, by Wanne J. Joe.
41. Webster's New Universal Unabridged Dictionary, second edition, definition #2.
42. *Korea's Cultural Roots*, Covel
43. *Spirit of the Mountains*, Mason
44. *Korean Heritage, Volume II*. Korean Overseas Information Service. 1996. Hollym International Corp., Elizabeth, NJ.
45. *Korea's Cultural Roots*. Covel,
46. *Spirit of the Mountains*, Mason

47. *Living Reed: A Novel of Korea*, by Pearl S. Buck 1963, Moyer Bell, NY
48. *Korea and Her Neighbours*. I.B. Bishop. p.340
49. *ibid.*, pp. 340, 341
50. *Wayfarer, New Fiction by Korean Women*, Edited and translated by B and J-C Fulton. 1997. Women in Translation, Seattle, WA.
51. *Korea's Cultural Roots*, Covell
52. *ibid.*, p. 459
53. My major resources for Korean historical information were the following books: *A Panorama of 5000 Years: Korean History* and *Introduction to Korean Cultural History* by Andrew C. Nahm; *A History of Asia* by Rhoads Murphy; and *Traditional Korea, a Cultural History* by Wanne J. Joe; for further details see Bibliography.
54. *Korea and her Neighbours*, Bishop, *ibid* pp. 180, 181
55. *ibid.* p. 449
56. *ibid*, p. 453
57. *ibid*, p. 454
58. *The Last Empress* is a musically fascinating dramatic opera, reputedly the first Korean musical opera in Western form, by, Yun Ho-jin (director), Kim Hee-gab (composer) and Yang In-ja (lyricist). I saw a performance at the Seoul Arts Center in the spring of 2000. As portrayed in the opera, American complicity in the Japanese takeover of Korea is obvious. This opera was also performed at the Lincoln Center's New York State Theater in 1997.
59. *Korea and Her Neighbours*. I.B. Bishop, p. 454
60. This is illustrated vividly and poignantly in Pearl S. Buck's novel, *Living Reed*, which, though fictional, incorporates factual instances of Japanese oppression during the occupation of Korea.
61. http://earthobservatory.nasa.gov/IOTD/view.php?id=79796
62. *The Two Koreas: A Contemporary History*, by Don Oberdorfer, a Northeast Asia correspondent for the Washington Post who lived in Korea for several years.
63. Map provided courtesy of the ReliefWeb Map Centre, UN Office for the Coordination of Humanitarian Affairs. It can be found online at: **http://reliefweb.int/map/republic-korea/korean-peninsula-provinces**

INDEX

A

ajuma 71, 72, 125
American military xi, xiv, xv, 4, 21, 28, 31, 35, 46, 66, 67, 81, 106, 139, 140, 143, 144, 147, 148, 164
Annyong hasseyo 103
Are you at peace? iii, xi, xiii, 89, 103

B

bar(s) 66, 70–72, 77, 142
Base Exchange 10, 18, 28
Bishop, Isabella xiv, 3, 4, 6, 7, 13, 14, 21, 22, 33, 34, 43, 44, 46, 53, 54, 56, 57, 59, 73, 75, 93, 101, 104, 107, 111, 115, 117, 118, 121, 126, 129, 145, 147–149, 155, 157, 159, 160, 167, 170
Bronze Age 152
Buck, Pearl 167
Buddha ix, 4, 5, 11, 57, 59, 61, 62
Buddhism 52, 116, 117, 119, 120, 122, 154
Buddhist monastery 93
Buddhist temple ix, 5, 6, 15, 30, 38, 52, 57, 58, 61, 63, 119, 120, 123, 138, 142, 149, 154
bulgogi 99, 130
buying a car 12

C

Camp Henry 67, 84, 87–89
Camp Hialeah 96
Camp Humphreys 13, 14, 15, 18–20, 24, 66, 68–70
Camp Long 46, 47, 48, 58, 125
Camp Walker 84, 87, 88
Catholic 157
Chang-an Sa 57, 93
Chejudo (Jejudo) ix, 33, 99, 100, 111, 165
China xi, xiii, 6, 32, 36, 41, 75, 92, 100, 104, 106, 119, 120, 144, 151–153, 154, 155, 157–163
Christianity 117, 121, 122, 130, 131, 156, 157
Christian(s) 114, 116, 117, 121–123, 157
Christmas 32, 91, 92, 114
Chusok 31, 90
commissary 10, 24, 28, 32, 66, 98
Confucian xiv, 22, 33, 64, 104, 105, 108, 121, 123, 125, 154
Confucianism 116, 117, 119–122, 154, 155
Confucius 58
contractor(s) xiv, 10, 24, 25, 27, 66, 73, 144
Covell, Jon Carter xii, 44, 118, 129, 167, 173
cranes 39, 44, 145

D

Demilitarized Zone 31, 33
Democratic People's Republic of Korea xiii, 35
Diamond Mountains 53–57, 75, 93, 116
DMZ ix, 31, 33, 34, 36–40, 101, 150
DPRK xiii, 34–36, 75, 163

E

East Sea 48, 49, 61
Emilie Bell 135
environment 21, 23, 28, 152

F

flood 75, 79, 82, 83, 147

G

gesang 127, 128
Gyeongju. *See* Kyongju

H

Han River 5, 44, 53, 93, 111
Hermit Kingdom xii, xiii, 1, 6, 148, 151

J

Japan xi, xiii, 1, 3, 4, 6, 32, 35, 41, 48, 72, 100, 104, 106, 144, 149, 151, 155, 159–162
Japanese xii, xiii, 3–6, 34–36, 49, 59, 61, 63, 75, 99, 101, 106, 107, 115–117, 122, 127–129, 135, 139, 144, 145, 147, 151, 152, 154–156, 158–161, 163, 175
juicy girls 70, 134

K

kim-bap 99
kim-chi 8, 9, 98, 130, 132, 133, 142

Kimpo Airport 26, 28, 125
King Kojong 34, 158, 160
King Sejong 107, 155
Kipling, Rudyard 73, 151
ko-chu-chang 98, 130
Koguryo 119, 120, 153, 165
Korea and her Neighbors xii, 3, 43, 53, 101, 126, 145, 159
Korean children 26
Korean culture 14, 21, 29, 101, 104, 108, 119, 128
Korean Folk Village 6, 120
Korean history 4, 6, 35, 37, 149, 151, 152, 154, 163, 168, 175
Korean language 10, 29, 52, 74, 80, 84, 104, 105, 107, 108, 144, 152, 156, 159, 161
Korean names 112, 165
Korean ponies 7, 54
Korean War xiii, xv, 3, 5, 14, 33, 36, 38, 59, 67, 83, 106, 129, 138, 139, 143–145, 149, 151, 152, 154, 163, 167, 173, 174
Korean women 15, 26, 29, 51, 54, 63, 107, 125, 127–131, 135, 144, 167, 174, 175
Koryo Kingdom 120, 154–156
Kunsan 96, 165
Kyongju ix, 58–62, 65, 67, 98, 111, 136, 149, 153, 165

M

MacArthur, General 3, 5, 36, 59, 162
Manchuria 33, 35, 47, 75, 144, 153, 161
Mason, David 49, 52, 118, 167, 168, 170
Methodist 157
missionaries 1, 21, 73, 116, 121, 122, 156, 157
misunderstanding 20, 109, 132
Mongol 152, 154, 155

monk(s) ix, 5, 52, 56, 58, 62, 116, 119, 120, 124, 136
monsoon 41, 74, 74–77, 81, 91
monsoon Asia 74, 75
mountains ix, 41, 43, 44, 46–50, 52–60, 61, 75, 93, 96, 97, 114, 116–119, 138, 139, 142, 145–147, 149, 150, 167, 174, 175
mutang 118, 129

N

Nature worship 117, 119
North Korea xi, xiii, xv, 33–35, 37–39, 53, 74, 144, 147, 150, 153, 162, 163
North Korean nuclear program 37

O

ondol heating 92, 93
Osan 4, 9, 10, 12–15, 18, 19, 23, 24, 26, 28, 31, 32, 37, 46–48, 51, 66, 67, 68–70, 76, 78, 80–84, 123, 130, 131, 139
otoshe 125

P

pajeon 99
Park Geun-hye v, 128
parking 13, 48, 62, 68, 85–88, 139
Pass and ID 67, 68, 69
Presbyterian 116, 157
Pulguksa ix, 61, 111, 124, 165
Pusan 3, 5, 14, 19, 21, 35, 59, 75, 84, 96, 111, 143, 144, 149, 162, 165

Q

Queen Min 34, 115, 158, 160

R

red pepper(s) 8, 9, 98, 138, 142, 148

religion 52, 101, 114–116, 119–121, 123, 130, 154
Republic of Korea xi, xiii, 35, 162, 164
ROK xi, 24, 35, 71
Russia xiii, 35, 37, 149, 159–161

S

San-shin 52, 53, 118, 167, 174
Sea of Japan 48
Seoul xii, 4–6, 12–14, 19, 24, 26, 28, 35–37, 43–45, 67–69, 72, 75, 84, 111, 119, 126, 131, 139, 143–145, 148, 159, 160, 162, 167, 169, 173, 175
Shamanism 115–119, 129
shaman(s) 52, 115, 115–118, 129, 136
Silla Kingdom (also Shilla Kingdom) 57, 58, 60, 98, 119, 135, 149, 153, 154
snow ix, 91, 92, 95, 114
SOFA 24, 25, 32, 67, 82, 88
Sohak 121, 157
Sokkuram ix, 61, 165
Songtan ix, 4, 8–10, 13, 18, 20, 31, 46, 51, 70, 72, 77, 80, 82, 83–85, 92, 94, 98, 114, 123, 131, 134, 139, 141
Son sang nim (very honored person) 64
South Korea xi, xiii, xiv, xv, 3, 4, 33–38, 99, 101, 111, 114, 128, 138, 147, 150, 162–164
students 24, 27, 28, 31, 51, 69, 134, 137
Suwon 36, 48
syncretism 114

T

Taegu ix, 24, 61, 67, 72, 76, 77, 79, 81, 84–89, 92, 93, 95, 96, 98, 99, 108, 123, 131, 132, 134, 145, 165
Taoism 116–119
Teacher 4, 26, 28, 29, 64, 112
Three Kingdoms 119, 120, 153
Tonghak (Tong-hak) 157, 165
tunnels beneath the DMZ 38, 39
turtle ships 156

U

UMUC Overseas Program 21
University of Maryland University College xi, 23, 123, 169
USSR xiii, 35, 36, 71, 152, 161, 163

V

village ix, 6, 7, 15, 16, 22, 37, 44–46, 72, 74, 76, 93, 113, 116, 120, 127, 138, 142, 146, 147, 149

W

Wonju 36, 46, 48, 52, 58
World War II xi, xiii, 35, 106, 144, 147, 151, 152, 161

Y

yamen 45, 105
yangban ix, 22, 45, 58, 104, 105, 107, 108, 113, 116, 120, 121, 123, 126, 147, 155, 156
Yi Dynasty 57, 119, 120, 149, 155
Yi Sun-sin 156
Yo-ju 45, 46
Yongsan 28, 67, 69, 72, 81, 131

Sketch of Korea, indicating routes taken by Isabella Bishop (circles), and places visited by the author (squares). The eastern Taebaek mountains split into two ranges near the middle of the peninsula. Flags of North Korea (above) and South Korea (below).

Made in the USA
Lexington, KY
01 September 2013